Debunk's

ILLUSTRATED GUIDE TO

The
Canadian Establishment

Valerie Rosedale
(Don Harron)

Debunk's

ILLUSTRATED GUIDE TO

The Canadian Establishment

BY DON HARRON
WITH MARTHA HARRON

ILLUSTRATED BY GRAHAM PILSWORTH

MACMILLAN OF CANADA
A Division of Gage Publishing Limited
Toronto, Canada

This book is dedicated to two dedicated women: my editor, Anne Holloway, who takes the words right out of my mouth and makes them look better on paper, and my firstborn, Martha, without whom this book would not have been possible.

CANADIAN CATALOGUING IN PUBLICATION DATA

Harron, Don, date.
   Debunk's illustrated guide to the Canadian establishment

ISBN 0-7715-9804-1

1. Elite (Social sciences)—Canada—Anecdotes, facetiae, satire, etc. 2. Capitalists and financiers—Canada—Anecdotes, facetiae, satire, etc. I. Pilsworth, Graham, 1944-
II. Title.

PS8565.A78D4   1984   305.5′2′0971   C84-099033-2
PR9199.3.H376D4   1984

DESIGN: Brant Cowie/Artplus
Printed in Canada

Contents

Fore Word

BY CHARLIE FARQUHARSON

That's all they ast me to rite, them eddyters at Debunk's. Fore word about the relayshuns the wife and I has down to Tronto in the high mucky-muck area of town. So I rit down the fore word: "Them ritches is differnt." Wernt good enuff, the pubelisher sed. First off, sumbuddy name of Effscotch Fitsgeritol rit the same blame thing yeers ago. Second off, fore words in books is spose to run on fer a cuppla pages. Shows yuh the power of inflayshun.

To begin at our beginning, us Farquharsons immigrunted here from Ireland in yer forties—not yer 19 but yer 18 forties. We got kick out of Ballyhilly in yer County Antrum by the same bunch had boot us outta Scotland a cuppla sentrys earlier, them overlard Anglican Saxaphones. They didden want us pessants on their land; they wanted sheep, on accounta yuh kin skin them morn once. So we hung round Ireland fer a hunnert yeers tryna grow potaters, but the hole country got over-run with them same blame absentee Anglish landlards. This time they wanted to stop plantin potaters, and it look like they was aimin fer to plant Farquharsons insted. So that's why we lit out fer Uppity Canada, yer boat peeple of a sexysintenniel ago.

So Valry Rozedale and me cum from common incesters, and wen we started we wuz all in the same boat. Wen her fokes left Ireland there wernt no lace curtins on ther shanty eether, and they kep the pig in the house jist like everybuddy elts. So how cum over here in Canada, where there's sposed to be no clash sistern and we're all cremated equal, that this Rozedale woman is close to yer tops while Charles Ewart Farquharson is scrapin bottoms?

Accorn to yer Theery of Elevation, we wuz all dropt offa the same family tree, but it looks like sum of us got more winded by the

7

fall. Seems to me I bin pritty close to yer ground ever since, wile this Valry woman, with the same roots as mine, is sociably climin her way back up that tree.

Now I got no mind to be among caféteria sassiety downtown with my name in yer Socialist Register. But I jist wonder how our branch of our family tree ends up tryna scratch a livin wile our city cussin sits around eatin canopys offen a tray and drinkin cavvyar. I know we're sposed to be content with our lot in life, but sumtimes I wish mine wernt so darn far north. Mebby the trubble start wen us Farquharsons got off the boat and rushed off in all drekshuns. I dunno why my grate granfather hedded strait fer the lumbar regions, becuz that stuff run out after a few ginrations, and we bin outa our tree on our land fer quite sum time.

I gess Valry's bunch didden move too much when they got offa the boat. They hung around Yorkvile, witch is what Tronto was call at the time. Not too much goin on down there in them daze, jist a few tooriests windershoppin as they stared at everybuddy's but-teeks. The mane action seem to be over on Jarvis Street and that's wher Valry's fokes open a meet market speshulizing in tender loins. They don't menshun that parta ther famly history much, but Valry gits downrite boastfull wen she tells about her gramma bein one of the founderers of a place fer wayword girls call Hav-a-Gal Callitch. It musta bin kinda a haffway house, becuz as soon as Jarvis Street started gettin fulla rundown peeple they mooved uptown lickety-spit. The "Condemm" sine was put up in front of the old billding by yer Bored of Helth and in no time it was bot up by them Canajun Broadcastering Commontaters, hoo have bin tryna prop up the condemm place ever since.

Everybuddy elts move northa Bloor Street fer to git away frum it all. That's wen this place Rozedale start up I gess. Now, cussin Valry is one of them, even tho she was *knée* (pardon my French) a Farquharson. I dunno wether her husbin's peeple name the place Rozedale or name therselfs after the place, but I suspek that after bein with that Jarvis crowd, they change their name so's they cood git a fresh start movin into a hireclass naberhood. I mind last time we had a famly re-onion was jist afore World War One, and its the oney time I ever got to meet any kin of them Rozedales, and they turn out to be mostly old Coots and Ferries. Charles Rozedale (that's his name, witch makes me, I spose, the udder Charlie), his mother was one of yer old Ottawa Coots, and his father was an old

Toronto Ferrie. Now yer Coots and yer Ferries is offshoots of yer Farquharson klansmen, so that'd make Mr. and Miz Rozedale first cussins to themsels. No wonder they looks so much alike, give er take his wallrust mustash. They say breeding tells, and inter-marge sure shows on the faces of our family.

But the thing that reely sticks up my craw is that both them uses this made-up name of Rozedale fer to cover up their backgrounds. And yet whenever there's a Rabbi Burns nite or Sin Andrews Balls, the both of them is out there shakin a boot and wavin ther Farquharson kilt, him in a minny and hern a maxy. Resta the yeer she never menshuns that she is reely an old Farquharson. I bleeve she was also a Leitch on her mother's peeple's side.

Do you know the mane differnts atween yer rich and yer poor? Bein rich don't take up all yer spare time. I dunno wat kinda deel them Rozedalers has pull off with their Mare, but that sluburb is the oney one in the hole of yer Metrapoppolitan Tronto that dont have to run ther garbitch out to the frunt twice a week, but kin leeve it to be clected in behind their backhouses. If anybuddy elts tried that they'd be up to heer in awful in no time.

And do you know wat reely gits my dandruff up? Mosta these urbane plutocraps becomes country gentilemen on weak ends, by buyin up good farmland and doin nothin with it but a little horsin around on the side and raisin a lotta Cane in ther leesure time. And wat's it all fur? So's that in November they kin show off their animal pets down to yer Royls Winterfare on Exhibitionist grounds at yer Hores Paliss nex to yer Colossalsemen. They puts on pink coats and plug hats and jumps over fensus in the big ring tryna git into their cups. If you ast me it's jist a buncha horses showin ther arses to a buncha horses arses showin ther horses.

Fore word? Looks more like fore page! And I still haven't sed my fore word about my Uppity Canajan cussins. How 'bout "The ritch is indifferent"? The wife and former sweethart, Valeda, she thinks that's sour gripes, on accounta Valry Rozedale takes a cuppla dozen of our aigs regler every other weak, and pays me fer haulin her ashes, blowin her snow, and cleenin her sceptic tank at her summer place up yer Go Home Bay. But that's the differnts atween yer country mouse and yer town rat. We hasta hussle fer to make our ends meat, and them high mucky-mucks jist has to sit ther watchin their tickers tape and clippin ther coopons. As a aggravacultured worker I feel sumtimes like I'm yer vanishin Canajun. I aint exactly on the outs with the resta sassiety but I sure am a long ways frum beein in.

So it kinda sprise me wen they ast me to innerduce this richbook and stick my feetnotes in whenever I seen fit to foot. I get credit fer havin horse sense becuz I've never ever had enuff money on me fer to make a fool of myself. As the Good Book sez about my middle ages: "In the midst of life we are in debt." But I'll be stickin my ore in other places too, givin youse a wormy eye view of the rich birds of this country, and how they feather ther nests, mostly frum crums like you and me.

Mind you, this book is about yer ladybirds that pervides yer nesteggs, and mebby they shooda got the wife and farmer sweethart fer to do the job insted. But don't worry, she'll be lookin over my sholder to see I'm givin the old gals a fare shake.

So if money is the root of all evil, then wat is the root of all money? Everybody wants to make the stuff, but the rich makes money with money, and if they has lotsa money then they makes lotsa money. Sure the ritch is differnt, but what's the differents? *"The Rich Has Credit."* That's my fore word. And in this book they gits credit for everything.

Sined

Charlie

CHARLES EWART FARQUHARSON THE 1st
(and last, probly)

10

*A Silly Old Boy going "strait" after a near-fatal bout of
philanthropy*

Valerie's dictum on marriage among the Canadian Establishment: "A little goose, a quick pluck, and the quill is gone."

Preface

BY VALERIE ROSEDALE

*W*hen Debunk's informed me of their intention to publish an illustrated guide to the illustrious Establishment of Canada, quite frankly I was mortified. We Established Canadians have always carried on under an afghan of anonymity, and we shrink to have our members exposed. Admission to the inner circle of the Establishment is by embossed invitation only. Only those who hold the keys to the kingdom know where the keyhole is. Until recently, few outsiders even suspected the existence of the Old Girls' Network that is the backbone of this country's body politic.

Unfortunately, Establishment-watching has become a national obsession of late, and the Old Boys' Network is no longer playing by the rules. Many of our Distaffers* have already suffered from glossy, off-colour exposure, thanks to their snap-happy husbands. The S.O.B.s* seem actually to *enjoy* it, and you will find them lying supine on their hard-cover spines, spread out on the coffee tables of the *nouveaux riches*,* and even the not-so-*riches*, from Victoria to St. John's. It is not a pretty sight.

In the past, we never paid the slightest attention to the nonsense being disseminated about us by the Johnny-come-recentlies of the so-called popular press, but now this drivel has swelled into a veritable torrent of misinformation. What Debunk's proposed to me was an insider's view of the Canadian Distaffestablishment, a personally guided tour down the corridors of privilege and up the back stairs of power. I blanched at the thought. I knew that it was

---

*Yer distaff is a stick spindlers uses fer woolgatherin and it keeps them wound up all the time. That's why it has became to meen sex of yer oppsit kind.

*Silly Old Boys.

*There's only three classes of money peeple: yer haves, yer have-nots, and yer have-not-paid-yet-fer-what-they-haves.

vitally important that this responsibility should not be placed in the wrong hands. Under the circumstances I felt compelled to adopt a missionary position. I had no choice but to accept the post of editor-in-chief of this volume.

What follows in this book is fact, not fiction. Only the names have been changed in the interests of feminine protection. The Old Girls' Network has exerted a staggering influence over local, national, and international affairs, made possible by its very anonymity. I am making the personal sacrifice of coming out of the closet, but I would never stoop to exposing any of my fellow members without their permission. Discretion is still the better part of Valerie.

I can only say that I deeply regret that constraints to my timetable have forced me to fall back on the assistance of my *very* distant relative, Charles Ewart Farquharson, to provide me with introductions to each of the provinces represented by a prominent Dynasty Clubber. I have made it clear to the editors at Debunk's that I can bear no responsibility for Mr. Farquharson's egregious lapses of taste, or for anything else he might do or say. Blood may be thicker than water, but in the unfortunate case of Mr. Farquharson and myself, the blood's of two very different and non-complementary colours.

As to the illustrated aspect of this guide, it is obvious that photographs were out of the question. In one click of the shutter, they would destroy anonymity and ruin carefully preserved profiles. Loose renderings by an artist seemed to be the only alternative, preferably by one of our own number. We found the right Old Girl for the job in Gram Pills-Worth. She has been trying to draw portraits all her life without success, none of them bearing the slightest resemblance to their subjects. Gram has graciously agreed to cross pens with me in this ignoble enterprise.

I also have to thank my daughter Stephanie for persuading me (by threatening to subscribe to *Toronto Life* magazine) to have the courage of my constrictions. She said it was high time someone lifted the veil of misconception that surrounds the female body politic. I agree. One can only take it lying down for so long.

Yours cordially

Valerie Rosedale

Editor-in-Chief

The Rosedale ancestors: Abernathy and Hilda on the right; the
other stuffed animals on the left.

An Old Girl always ends up carrying the can for some man.

I

The Powder Network

Patrolling the Perfumed Stockings of Canada's Establishment

From old St. John's on our eastern cheek to fair Victoria on the western, from Pelly Bay on our frigid fringe to hot Point Pelee on our temperate tip, the Canadian Establishment has woven an invisible network that blankets this country from shore to shore to shore to shore, and so forth. The result is such a cosy cover that an outsider wouldn't know if he had a member in his hand, let alone two in the bush.

The reigning queens of the Canadian Establishment's Old Girls' Network are known as the Powder Brokers, after the room in which their most private functions are performed. It is a compact so private, and so exclusive, that only those who belong to it know who they are, where they meet, and what they do. I won't lift the lid on what they get up to in there, but I can tell you that the Powder Room has been the inner sanctum of the female elite since before the dawn of recorded history.*

Back then, in the first Powder Room of the Chinese Imperial Court at Hwang Dong, the powder wasn't for the courtiers' noses—inside or out. Rather they had concocted it as a new kind of parlour game. The ladies of the court were quite proud of their pyrotechnics and delighted when the kiddies got a bang out of the first fireworks display. The thrill lasted until their husbands took the powder and started blowing up peasants. Since then the Powder Room has been strictly off-limits to the opposite sex.

The ladies decided to "forget" the recipe, and soon the powder lost its punch. They swore off volatile cocktails (although we still use plenty of charcoal and saltpetre for cooking) and resolved to stick to spinning, taking up the distaff as their symbol. The Imperial Order of the Distaff (I.O.D.) has had many spin-offs since

---

*In China—them Chinee have been in the recording business since at least 4000 B.C.B.C.**
Yer Chinee was ritin pomes on poorfumed paper wen we wuz all eetin raw meet in caves.
**Before CBC.

18

The Big Bang theory: the Old Girls' Movement started in the powder room.

its inception in 2670 B.C., but the Powder Brokers have never forgotten that it all started with a big bang. We make no apologies for the unisex status of the Old Girls' Network, because we know that any tool can become a weapon in the wrong hands, or as we say: "Give a man a distaff and he'll stick it to somebody."* You know how boys are: you breed them, you feed them, you dress them up and try to train them, but the minute your back is turned they're doing something nasty on the floor of the Exchange.

The New Woman tries to compete with men, but we Old Girls think of them as a means to an end. As the Honourable Ellen Fairclough once pointed out, "The battle of the sexes can never be won by either side. There is too much fraternizing with the enemy." Mind you, she was the first female Canadian cabinet minister, and I think that being closeted with that many private members at once is taking fraternization a bit too far.

Most of us Old Girls prefer a one-on-one situation, and that is why half of Canada's Establishment is of the masculine persuasion.* Our continued success depends upon mutual bonds between men and women for future issue. Budding Powder Brokers know that a good front man is worth his weight in gold, and they tend to marry bricks like their fathers. We Old Girls like a firm foundation. Likewise Establishment lads don't marry sports cars, they marry station wagons. Let's face it: comfort and reliability are far more important for the long haul than shiny paint and a monocoque chassis, if you want to avoid costly breakdowns. Marriage is a serious investment!

Establishment groupie Peter Parvenu seems to feel sorry for poor boys who marry rich girls, and calls Establishment wives "baubles" and "burdens" and "non-persons." He doesn't realize that we've been polishing our craven image ever since Adam tried to make Eve take the Fall for the bitten fruit! Thinking that the Old Boys are lumbered with a fifty-per-cent overhead, he considers the Establishment Man an endangered species, and studying this rare creature in its natural habitat has become his life's work. Mr. Parvenu can tell you where *homo establiens* lives, how he loves, what he wears, how he thinks, and where he spends his money. "When in London, does Establishment Man stay at Claridge's, or

---

*Not true. Sum of us men is patsyfists.
*We get this statisticull informayshun by cummin to our sensus.

"I thought, Val, that a ghetto blaster was a successful property developer, or I'd never have let Melissa have one."

the Connaught?" is a subject of endless discussion. (The answer, if you *must* know, is neither. Hotels are a waste of money. When abroad, we like to stay with family or friends. Frankly, any Establishment Man who can claim neither—in London of all places!—must have a few loose connections.)

New Money loves to spend; Old Money loves to save. How do you think New Money got to be Old Money in the first place? Watching the flash-in-the-pan antics of the *nouveaux riches* is one of the Canadian Establishment's favourite spectator sports. When the Pucklingtons peter out to a final flicker, and the Nelson Lusitanias go down for the last time, we'll pull out the deck-chairs and toast a fond farewell to the Foundering Fathers of Consolidation.

As soon as our first families arrived in Canada from Europe,* the Old Boys dug into fur, banking, and railroading the country. Later, some took to strip mining for nickel and dime deposits, while others drilled for oil and got gas. The Old Girls stuck to sugar and spice and everything on ice.

And then there was wampum. Obviously some of the first Old Girls must have reached the New World from the West Coast long before Queen Isabella sent Chris off in his craft. The trail of the Powder Network was unmistakable. Wampum has all the characteristics of the quintessential Old Girl gizmo: it's highly decorative, multi-functional, and top-secret, and folds perfectly for travelling.

The French girls called the beautiful purple and white beads *pourceline*, because they reminded them of the exquisite porcelain china back home. Jacques Cartier dubbed wampum *esnoguy*, for as he put it, "Es no guy could 'ave made such beautiful li'l balls!" Wampum beads made beautiful bracelets, necklaces, and medallions, but they were also strong medicine. They could stop a nosebleed on contact, which was a great boon to Cartier and his scurvy crew.

Evolved from the Chinese abacus, wampum beads were the native people's written language. Strung on belts, the order of white, purple, and purple-and-white beads told a tale, recording all important historical events and economic transactions. No treaty

---

*Rong. First familys of Canada cum frum yer Gobye Dessert in China soon as they got there Bearings Strait.

was complete without passing a couple of pipes and having a few belts.

Wampum was the only solid currency North America has ever had. Whites, natives, men and women, *everybody* swapped wampum, but no one seemed to know where it came from or how it was made. The legend was that the great Wampum Bird swooped down, shook its wings, and showered the ground with beads.* A likely story.

In fact, the native Old Girls had evolved a very complicated recipe using certain shells. Unfortunately, in 1621 a group of Italian workmen were imported to set up a glass-blowing factory in Virginia, and it wasn't long before they had flooded the market with counterfeit wampum. Some say it was the work of the Cosa Nostra, but we suspect it was the Hung League, ancient Chinese rivals of the Powder Brokers, rearing their ugly heads again.

Whoever was behind it, few newcomers could distinguish funny money from the genuine article, being ignorant of wampum's potent medicinal properties. The currency was debased, causing rampant inflation, and by the middle of the nineteenth century wampum had virtually disappeared from the open market—straight into the vaults of the Powder Network, where it has proved a marvellous hedge against inflation.* Considering the way the boys on the hill in Washington and Ottawa keep increasing their deficits, it won't be long before we're all back on the Wampum Standard.

The Powder Network has never pegged its fortunes to the price of gold, or the Canadian dollar, or any other common currency. Not only are these subject to government regulation and taxation, they are also, by extension, hopelessly unstable. Unlike politicians and the press, the Powder Brokers never waste any time trying to make the rest of the world share their values.

Many things of negligible cash value are worth their weight in wampum. These the Old Girls acquire. Items highly prized by the masses we unload on the *nouveaux riches*, who have far more money than they know what to do with anyway. The same holds true of the professions. The importance of a Powder Broker's occupation can usually be measured in inverse proportion to its

---

*I kin see where they got the ideer. That's why I always wears a hat.
*Meening them wimmen has all the balls?

23

remuneration. In other words, most of the executive positions draw no salary whatsoever. This is disparagingly referred to by New Money as "volunteer" work. We find it keeps the riff-raff away from the real action.

The greatest empire is as piffle before the wind without a successor capable of manning the helm and managing the crew. The children of the *nouveaux riches* have fame and fortune handed to them on a gilt platter. They don't know what they're missing. If they did, they would know that poverty is extremely unpleasant and well worth avoiding. Not understanding the value of what they possess, is it any wonder they throw principle to the wind?

The Canadian Establishment has evolved very successful methods for instilling discipline and determination in its children without personally mistreating them in any way. Celtic nannies* seem to be born with the proper degree of fond severity, but it can be acquired by others. Establishment babies are placed in harness right from the cradle: this prevents them from flipping onto their backs (a habit that stays with Old Girls for life, and discourages some Old Boys from snoring).

The next step is school. How fondly I remember my own Loathsome Hall days. I'm not going to tell you what the "right" schools are now, because you might send your children there, but a few pointers might be in order. Coeducation is out of the question, of course. Competition for the young belongs on the playing field, not in playing the field. Fashion is a distraction, so school uniforms are a must. Basic academic subjects must be studied, however unstable the instructor. Outdoor games are just as important, no matter how dismal the weather. These experiences build character.

Creative curriculum is best left to after-hours. Idle hands are the devil's playground, as they say, so one can't have too many extracurricular activities. Voice, dulcimer, clarinet, ceramics, weaving, ballet, and skating are good for girls; cricket and hockey for boys; and piano, dance, and abacus for everybody can usually get you through the school year without too much difficulty. Chauffeuring of course becomes a part-time job, for which Mother is amply unpaid.

---

*Does she meen Scotch gotes?

Labour Relations

Horsemanship

Social Studies

It is important that the children do these things often, but not necessarily well. Our job is to produce patrons, not painters. The long hours of practice will make them into an appreciative audience, and they won't clap in the middle of a movement when you take them out for some tea and symphony.

During school breaks, the young should be taken north to ski in blizzards, or south to sail in icy gales, preferably in the company of their fathers, because Mummy says it's fun. Like dogs, children are best kept out of doors as long as the light holds. Summers are usually evenly divided between cottage and camp. The right sort of camp can be very expensive, but we view it as a worthwhile investment. It must have the four Cs—chapel, campfire, cabin, canoe—and precious little else. You don't know the meaning of fun until you've survived a ten-day canoe trip, singing, paddling, burning all day, freezing all night. The bears eat your food, and the blackflies eat what's left of you during the five-mile portages. When you get back, if you're *really* lucky, Miss Midcalfe ("Windiehaha") will tell you some of her Indian tales. By that point, the little darlings are grateful just to be alive.

The wrong sort of camp is cheaper, but the price includes electricity, hot and cold running water, flush toilets, central heating, scuba-diving, water-skiing, tennis, movies, video games, good food, a shopping mall, and ample opportunity to consort with the opposite sex. Fortunately the wrong sort of people all send their children to the wrong sort of camp, because the *nouveaux riches* just don't understand value for money.

Upon coming out, graduating, and finishing (usually in that order), it is time for the young tads to leave home and begin the business of earning a living. This does them a lot of good, especially those who may never have to do it again. Renting a practice nest with other fledglings of similar gender is an invaluable education in itself. No man/woman relationship could survive the experience.

Once professionally launched and reasonably house-broken, the young cocks and hens are ready to begin the serious business of pair-bonding and nest-building, generally in the expectation of several eggs. Of course not all graftings bear fruit, and sometimes this is a blessing.

Being *homo sapiens* rather than simple cockatoos, some of us prefer not to pair off at all. Without maiden aunts and uncles, the world would indeed be a dull place. One visit from Great-Aunt

"My daughter Stephanie loved her stay at Camp Kilimanjaro,"
says Valerie Rosedale.

*The young pets of the Canadian Establishment must be
paper-trained early in life.*

Gertrude at Christmas will draw the most distant relatives together and furnish enough amusing anecdotes to last until Easter. Weddings are mergers, and require a great deal of careful planning. After that, the New Old Boy must grapple long hours in his chosen field, while the New Old Girl begins the long series of thankless tasks required to earn her place in the Powder Network.

Apart from raising a husband and family, these tasks usually include shifts at the Op Shoppe selling second-hand clothes for the Junior League, school committees, fund-raising for culture and charity, entertaining hubby's endless procession of professional colleagues, mastering the intricacies of having lunch, then onward and upward to the Bridge Club, the Golf Club, the Book Club, the Investment Club, and, finally, the Garden Club.

We are often told that life begins at forty. Not necessarily. For some it begins when the last child leaves college; for others, when the first grandchild comes to visit. Grandparents can break all the rules they set as parents. As they ripen, the fruits of the Establishment tree are allowed to fall where they may. The sky's the limit, as they say, provided the risk is your own. This the middle classes call eccentricity. Perhaps. We say life is like lunch: eat what's put in front of you, then have whatever you want for dessert.

"When I want a footman, Val, I want a footman."

II

The Dynasty Club

An Introduction to the Dynasty Club

Scaling the peaks of the Powder Network is a long, hard climb. Those gallant Old Girls who make it to the top, the *crème de la crème* of the Distaffestablishment, are issued into that noble sisterhood known as the Dynasty Club.

Of course most Powder Brokers come from the right sort of family and go to the right sort of school, but any girl who has "the right stuff" can rise through the ranks. Most members of the Dynasty Club today are self-made women. Never let it be said that we Old Girls run a closed shoppe.

The Dynasty Clubbers of Canada, the Great Dames who hold this country together under the leadership of our head girl, the Imperial Great Dame herself, have hitherto managed to avoid public exposure. This is the first time in history that they have agreed to be interviewed as a body, and it may be the last. It is with great pride, therefore, that I introduce them to you here.

*When teed-off with men, we Old Girls enjoy trying out a few of
our basic drives.*

NoFunland

*I*wunder if the name of this place will have to be change to NoFunland after the Spreem Cort gits thru with it? The place seems to be fulla a lotta Ayatoleyuhs running around these days sayin "Ayatoleyuh we shunt have jined up with Canada back in '49!"

Mind you the place ain't bin self-servicing since yer urly thurtys. After that it was repossess by yer Birdish and the hole place went on the pogey. It wernt nobody's province then but a Dumb Minion all on its own. Now it feels the same way about bein hitched up to Ottawar.

It celibated its four hundredth berfdy not too long ago, and all that time watever guvmint's bin in power has run it on yer middle-age futile sistern. This is a two-class leeg with eether ritches or poors and nobuddy in between. The poor ye shall always have with ye, accorn to the Good Book, but they never git invited in. Oh, took in, yes, but not ast to stay fer supper.

Durin the war, Newfunland was part of yer U.S.O. and peeple got so used to Americans that a little broadcasterater name of Joey Smallwood thot that they cood mebby git used to Canajuns too. So he start up a one-man croosade fer to git his berthplace anex to yer

maneland, so's he cood becum the oney livid Father of Conflagra-
tion. He tole his fella inhibitants that there was sumthin fishy
about their economy, and that they shood all fold their nets and
silently steel away frum their outports and join the twennieth
senchery in the big-time towns.

Twenny yeers later, Joey's big cry was "Power to the Peeple,"
but wen it cum to Churchle's Falls it turnd out he ment power to
the peeples of Cuebeck, and they've bin turned on by his cheep
killerwats ever sints. Mebby Joey shood have inclood a high cost of
keepin-up-livin claws in the contrack, so's his bunch wood by now
be gittin the index insted of the finger.

Anuther big projeck has bin yer oil off yer shore. So far this has
bin nothin but a brag, a groan, and a tank of air. The Spreem Cort
made the final blow off the merang on ther pie in the sky wen it sed
that all that oil, if it cums up ever, blongs to yer Federasts guvmint.
I think Newfunlanders shood go back to catchin fish. It's workin
fer scales, but at leest yuh kin put it on the table cum suppertime.

a·mari·usque·ad·mare·

Cyril and "Splits" tried to keep their marriage mum.

Splits! The very nickname brings back those dear dead days almost beyond recall at Miss Edgar's and Miss Cramp's School for "Gells" in Montreal back in 1949. Our families sent us there, I do believe, in the vain hope that we would all end up bilingual. *Petite chance de cela*, with all of us Anglos clumping together and the Pollywogs ensconced in their own compound. I opted for grass hockey instead of conversational French, because Mummy felt it better form to show grass stains on one's knees than on one's back.

How we Cramp girls would laugh like drains at the antics of Splits Puddock, the little token Newf who tended nets. I always thought her sobriquet referred to the weird gyrations she made as she thrashed about saving the honour of our House and fending off attackers at her goal mouth. The Pollys of Edgar House dubbed her "La Dame" Splits because this was the only intelligible English word they ever heard her say.

But the secret of Splits's nickname was revealed when Newfoundland became our tenth province. Poor Puddock was in deep funk for weeks after that event. "Splits" is a Down East word for small pieces of wood, and the dear girl was simply cursing Premier Joey for allowing the mainland of Canada to join him in this wretched Confederation.* This union would bring in such outlandish institutions as Eaton's and Simpsons to create an unwanted diversion and harass the merchants of St. Johns' Water Street, namely the Puddocks.

Upon graduation *minima cum laude* Splits set to work to form a De-Confederation Party on the island, and achieved some success in recruiting during weekends on St. Pierre and Miquelon. Although the undercover operation goes on, her main covert campaign is to

---

*There was quite a screech made when Smallwood let Canda jine up with Newfland, and the natives have bottled it up ever sints.

undo the Smallwood legacy by reviving the far-flung outports, those last resorts of marine life. This emphasis on net profits for the small family fish-bowl as opposed to the federally subsidized megaconglomerate has caused her to be considered an atavistic throwback to a pre-Confederation never-never-again land, an odd-fishball in the *bouillabaisse* of the St. John's social set. "I have seen the past, and it works!" she hoots triumphantly.

Let there be no mistake, there is sea water in those Puddock veins, with more than a lump of ice. The family migrated from Devon to Labrador donkey's centuries ago, floundering for generations until their last anchor man, Great-Granddad Gurry Puddock, tied a granny instead of a reef and went down on his Salt Banker to the great Jiggin' Ground in the Sky. Great-Gran Puddock, the codmother of the clan, decided that they should bank on something else by marketing fish instead of catching it. Rather than live a life in Nain, she moved them all, lox, sox, and chattels, to Water Street, St. John's, to learn the ABCs of the retail trade (Aird, Bowring, Crosbie *et al.*).

Splits's netting of Cyril Noseworthy in '51 was considered the season's catch. Ledgerwise, I suppose, it's true. The Noseworthys have had a provisioner's licence for outfitting the British fleet since the first Elizabeth set up throne. It was during the other glorious reign, Victoria's, that the Noseworthys gave up piracy on the high seas for the same well-grounded tradition on Water Street.

The matrimonial merger of Puddock and Noseworthy took place at St. Michael and All Anglers, and after the usual Bermuda break-in period, the newlyweds moved into Cyril's family vault, a mock Queen Anne woodpile of gloom on Circular Road, which is not really circular at all but is so called because the residents take delight in giving each other the run-around.

Run-around is a word frequently found on the lips of Newfound-landers these days. Splits says that when she was a minnow at her mother's knee, the dream of every upper-class family on the Rock was to go to London and be presented at court. But ever since Prime Minister Trudeau went to London and came back with our brand new constitution, the Ottawa court is deemed to be supreme over the one at Buckingham Palace.

This Canadian court of last resource has certainly been stripping Newfoundland of its natural heritage. To most Newfoundlanders, losing a case usually means misplacing one's beer, but to the few families who control the economy of the island, those men in the long red frocks in Ottawa have succeeded in taking the wind out of all their sails.

"You see, Val, dear," confided Splits as we watched the tall ships sail by, "one problem of living in the lap of luxury is that one never knows when the lap is going to stand up." This seems to happen to the Puddock tribe every ten years, she says. In 1949 (on April Fool's Day, appropriately enough) Joey Smallwood dragged Ida "Splits" Puddock into Confederation. Immediately she became the island's only active separatist. Home from the holidays from Miss Cramp's, she would stalk up and down in front of the Legislature with a sign reading "Joe Must Go And So Should Us'n!" She became a standing joke at Cuckold's Head cocktail parties with her insistence on looking through Smallwood's rose-coloured glasses with a jaundiced eye. But her fellow islanders laugh no longer; now she is considered a hawk in budgerigar feathers, and not a few are flocking to her colours.

Nineteen fifty-nine was the year of the Quiet Revolution in Quebec. ("It could never happen here, Val," she says confidently. "Everybody would make such a racket!") Whatever happened in 1969 between Smallwood and Lesage when they sat down at the table at Churchill Falls made the old Bible prophecy come true: "Ye were a stranger and I took you in." Actually my token Québécoise friend Mazo Laroque-Fortier says it's not quite true. The negotiations were done by two corporations, a public one for Quebec and a private one for Newfoundland, and only after Joey had tried to get some big U.S. investor (Alcan or Alcoa or Coca-Cola, I forget which) to put some money in the kitty. It was Quebec who took a chance on their power grid lottery and won. I'll leave Mazo and Splits to fight it out. I think that business people shouldn't waste their time in politics (that Mulroney boy is so stubborn) when the business of business is minding your own.

Speaking of politics, 1979 was the year Brian Peckford quit school and became premier, and told Newfoundlanders they would soon be rich beyond their dreams. His fellow citizens went on a big high. They've been on it ever since, according to Splits Puddock: "Highest income tax, highest public debt, highest unemployment, highest sales tax!" As she raves on, her voice loses the quality of Miss Edgar's and Miss Cramp's and takes on those of the squid-jigging ground.

I asked her what alternative there was for her beleaguered province. Union with Britain or the U.S.? "Niver!" she roars and rants like a true Newfoundlander. "We shall form the sovereign state of Newfoundland and Labrador: Newflab!" I had visions of a vast fat farm from Cape Race to Wabush, but Splits is deadly serious about the future of her island home. Putting a burglar alarm on the garbage can is no longer a Newfy joke. "We're out in the cold again, Val, hon. Just like the history books always said, we're nothin' but whores of the woods with our drawers full of water!"

Splits and Cyr have been blest with issue too numerous to mention here, but the distaff side is well represented by daughter Daff, who keeps Mummy informed on the doings of the oily slickers in the cartels from her post in the P.M.O.* Hubby Cyr has been eased ever so slightly sideways out of his exec chair and his hindquarters now repose most of the time at the Murray Pond Club. Dear Splits is like as not to be nearby, but on the pond itself, dressed in her oilskin foulies and doing a bit of social gaffing. Last year at West Palm she pulled in hubby's weight in marlin, and next summer she heads for Baffin hoping to catch grayling over the railing near Pang. Cyr wants to tag along as bait, but I.O.D. meetings loom on the tundra, so dear Cyr will be left home with the garden shears to clip his coupons.

While Cyr still thinks the future of Newfoundland is in oil, Splits opts for fish. I have heard her tell her hub more than once at the dinner table: "One spill and yer out!" Later over midnight snackies she sounded her credo once again as we opened a tin of sardines: "Oil and fish don't mix!"

---

*Got to meen "Precedent of Mobil's Office," of which we are a blanched plant.

The Old Girls find that good breeding keeps them off their feet.

Prints Ed Ilund

*I*t was first call "A Big White" by yer Mixmax injuns in onner
of Jack Carter, hoo first cum upon them four hunderd yeer
ago with his (fer them Injuns) too tall ships. This place used
to be yer Garden of Eatin, becuz jist about anything grew here.
Now it is rejuice to a one-crap economy, and I don't meen pertaters.
Them intynashnuls is movin in on yer lokels *à la cartel*. Most
farmers keeps a chick or two on the side, and mebby a hawg but
there's gittin to be no place fer the slotter. The Candapackers plant
is own by the Charlatan guvmint, and hawgs don't git kilt the same
day they cum in, as promised, but hang around over the weekend
and loose mebby five pound in wate. (They say it's water, but I
know yer pigs and I take that with a dose of salt.) Artifishul
insinuation is in a bad way too, and farmers are still waitin fer a nite
depossetory on ther sperm bank. A Milk Markupping Bored is
leevin farmers out in the cold in the derry air and it has bin
boycocked by yer N.F.U. (witch sounds rude but is reely yer
Nashnul Farmers' Union). Yer Japanee fakefish is scallopin the
homegroan catch by cuttin prices in haff. The guvmint promised to
lend a sinthetic eer but so far nothin has happen.

So what's the crap I'm a talkin bout? It's importin tooryists,
that's what. That's about it fer this Iland, apart frum bein yer

hindquarters fer the D.V.A. shunists in charge of the Vetruns Having Affaires. They tried to raze a few bucks fer the vets by givin them danger pay on accounta ther Iland is morn six mile offen yer maneland, and if yer morn three mile out to sea, that puts yuh in a wore zone. It's a good thing they never bilt that cozway or them old swetts at yer Leegend wooden be gittin this extry beer munny. I never thot P.E.I. was the beeches Winsome Churchle was talkin about, with his blud, swett, and beers, but turns out they was sum of them Nasty slubmarines about at the same time as we was assalting yer ramsparts on Beeday in 1944. I wud a thunk there was more danger over to Hallyfacks durin them VeeDeeJayday riots than you wouda found round the hole circuminterference of Prince Edward's Iland frum 1939 to 45. But why shunt our vets line up at the troff alonga side of everybuddy elts?

But that ain't gonna keep this Iland aflote. It's yer anual strangers that keeps comin back that is the big bananza they're lookin fer. And they keep bildin morn more toorist distractions. Like them minityer replickers of famous old piles like yer Excommunication Tower of London, wher peeples lost ther heds over yer crowned jools, and the Two Sods Mooseum where yer grate and yer neergrate is rendered down into wacks, and yer Stanley Britches Murine Mewseeyum of Stuffed Birds and Live Mounted Animals.

The new name fer this Iland is yer Garden of yer Golf, on accounta it's fulla peeple in loud close havin a few strokes chasin little balls into holes.

a·mari·usque·ad·mare·

Woolgathering in P.E.I. with your obedient servant, Shirley Anne McBlythe.

Shirley Anne "Carats" McBlythe

I do love a Cinderella story, don't you? And Shirley Anne's story is one of the romantic epics of all time, in any language. Born an orphan in Newfoundland and left on the steps of a foundling asylum near Carbonear, "Carats" has won the hearts and minds and pocketbooks of all her contacts. Raised in the asylum, and branded ever since as mentally unstable, Shirley Anne has turned out to be as crazy as the proverbial fox.

Farmed out initially into a series of foster homes in western Newfoundland, through a typographical error she landed in the pits of Cape Breton as a minor. When the misplaced vowel was discovered, she was about to be re-exported to Newfoundland when a call came from the Humane Society in Glace Bay: "Couple living out of Wedlock, P.E.I., desire Newfoundlander for sheep labour. Dog preferable." The social worker thought our Shirley Anne fit the bill, and so she was unleashed on the Island. Bert and Letitia Cavendish, the childless couple who took Shirley Anne in, tried several times to contact the Humane Society in Charlotte-town about the bureaucratic error. "Even an experimental Lab would have been worth a try with our sheep, but this is too much," Bert muttered in his beer.

But little Shirley Anne was determined to retrieve a place for herself in their lives. She was soon learning to fetch and carry sticks and round up strays. She placed honourable mention in the yearling trials at Alberton* and was given a scholarship to go to obedience school at Orwell Cove (P.S. 84). It was here that she acquired the nickname "Carats" by lying about her roots, claiming to be a kidnapped heiress kept in slavery until she revealed the where-abouts of the family jewels. This impressed no one, with the notable exception of Howard McBlythe, whose father owned the biggest cattle ranch on P.E.I. (approximately forty head). But

*Not the west province but a town to yer east and north of Charlatan.

45

cattlemen and shepherds (or shepherdesses) are traditional enemies, and that's how our Shirley Anne felt about Howard—until she saw his big house with the green gables, and the expanse of his plum orchards. She coveted these plums, thinking of herself as "Anne of Green Gages" from that day forth.

But how to make one's fortune on a tiny island where people had eyes only for their potatoes, and when even this staple was being taken over by outlandish interlopers? Prince Edward was becoming known as the Island God gave to McCain. The answer came in a blinding flash of bright lights on the night of the high school graduation of our little Carats and her "Big Stoop." She had given Howard this pet epithet when she first spied his huge front porch and envisioned herself standing on it encrusted with more jewels than a Swiss watch.

First came the graduation ceremony itself. Both Shirley Anne and Howard were close to the bottom of the class, but they had been too much wrapped up in each other to care (nights are cool on P.E.I.). There was a dance after at the Rodd Royalty Inn, but instead the pair of them slipped away for a familiar neck in the woods off the North River Road.* Just before the critical moment they were interrupted by a blinding light from a car that had pulled up behind them, and a nasal voice blared, "How far is yer Rodd Inn?" Howard was ready for fisticuffs as soon as he could adjust himself, but his bride-to-be understood the clarion call perfectly. *Tourism!* That was the only future for her adopted island. How right she was!

After Shirley Anne and Howard had consummated their union, they eventually married and immediately plunged into relative poverty.* Howard plugged away at his cattle and tried to amalgamate them with Shirley Anne's sheep, while diddling and dabbling even less successfully with not-so-live stocks in other markets.

Her former foster parents, the Cavendishes, pulled up stakes in 1979 and headed for Calgary, so Shirley Anne seeded their acres in sod, drilled eighteen holes, added some sand and a dune buggy, and used the old homestead for a clubhouse. Within weeks the little orphan girl overcame her initial handicap and scored a hole-in-one in an under-par economy. Next she opened a string of convenience

---

*Noan to the lokels as "Ruffing It in Yer Bush."
*This meens havin to live with yer fambly.

46

shops that stay open from seven in the morning until eleven at night. The nickname "Carats" has evoked a dream come true: she de-emphasizes her now fading titian hair with plenty of sparklers and oils her freckles with Oil of Olay each day, as she mines the nuggets of nostalgia.

The triumph of tourism over all else continues unabated on the Island. Anne is planning to de-horn Howard's cattle ranch and turn it into a pleasure park called Orphan Annieland, where all visitors, parents and children, can lose themselves in a never-never world of trivial pursuits. Howard complains that this is a part-time project, because tourists come to P.E.I. only in the summer, but Shirley Anne is more far-sighted. She plans to change the island's name to Greenland, tear down the fences, and make it the national headquarters for cross-country skiing.

For the moment, the exhausted but solvent little island counts its blessings the day after Labour Day and prepares to hibernate until the first sign of green peeks from the pockets of next season's tourists. "We have always depended on the kindness of strangers," muses the reigning patron saint of Prince Edward Island, Carats McBlythe.

A curtsy call on the multifaceted "Carats."

Novy Kosher

That song "Nova's Kosher Fares Well" seems to have live up to its name sept fer miner problems in Cape Breton. Mind you, nothin is on the table frum yer gas frum yer Sable as yit. Like posterity in yer thurtys, it seems to be jist around the corner and has bin fer quite sum time. Farteen yeer, smatter of fack.

These Marmtiders ain't ones to put on side and show it all off. The wife and I has relations down this way, and I never mind once runnin into a millyunair. I spose they exists, but mebby their too busy sellin groceries or slingin beer fer to take time to put on errs. Rich peeple down this way seems more like pore peeple hoo happen to run into money, like winnin yer Blotto Candida. Even if their chips cum in a long time ago, they don't seem to flounce ther welth too much.

Jist as well, fer they got ther share of nare-do-wells, but it's hard to tell yer welloff frum yer rundown indigment becuz they all acts so urthy and downhomey—even tho sum kin probly trace ther famly tree back to the time wen their incesters lived in it.

The mane differents with Newfinland is that yer Nosy Koshan has made a deel with the Federast guvmint over their offyershore resorses of yer Stable Iland. So far the only thing has bin brung up is gas, and a lotta septics think that the only oil out that way is to be found on the backs of them ponies. But nothin has cum up yet so far, sept fer one big blowout of a belch that hadda be cap by sum Texassans hoo are blowhard experks.

But Newfylanders thinks Novy Koshers dun a bad deel with Ottawar like they therselfs dun with Cuebec on yer hydra. Fer every dollar the Bluenosers erns frum oil er gas, they get dock a doller in equallyization transfer paymints ("on releef" it use to be call befor the sibble serpents fanceed the name up).

So what they gains on the swingers they loses on them roustabouts. It's like when I drinks my winter tonic, beef iron and wine. It bilds me up as it tares me down, and I genrully comes out even.

Moosie loves to hit the bottle over launch.

Cynthia "Moosie" Dawes Hedlund

Of course the great unwashed seem to think that "Moosie" Hedlund (*née* Cynthia Dawes) was labelled for her husband's bestselling beer, but she was dubbed Moosie donkey's years before she met Brucie Hedlund and became his head girl. In fact, dear little Cynthia was always called Moosie, even before she joined the Saraguay Club or attended Halifax Ladies' College. I thought perhaps it was her inordinate fondness for imported chocky desserts, but Cynth claims the epithet came from her old Scots nanny, who dubbed her small charge a "wee, wee moosie in a braw, big hoosie." I'm not sure about the braw bit, but she still lives in the big, big hoosie out in Boulderwood, built yare and square by her great-great-great-grandfather.

Josiah Dawes was the last man to build wooden ships, and to try to give Sam Cunard a run for his money. But the winds had changed; Cunard went ahead full steam on a subsidy, leaving his rival becalmed and muttering something about ship disturbers. The old Dawes homestead was actually saved from the bailiffs by Great[3]-Grandmamma Dawes, who took in sail and put her husband in dry-dock to repair the damages to his sobersides. It was the Dawes distaff side that provided the stitches in time for Natal Day and other amateur activities of the Royal Nova Scotia Yacht Squadron coupon-clipper set.

While his wife sewed what he had ripped, poor Josiah was often found without a stitch. Reduced to one brass-buttoned coat and a pair of nankeen trousers, he was sometimes forced to take to his bed while his sole outfit was in repair. More and more often he could be found pacing the widow's walk at the top of the house, clad in nothing but a pink gin and one of his wife's frocks. He became a bit of a drag after that.

Ever since, the Dawes girls have retained a reputation for hijinks in all fields, and sometimes on beaches. Moosie must have quarts of old Josiah's salt water in her veins because, even after getting the

Hedlund lock on Bruce, she insisted on staying out on the Northwest Arm, despite her hub's entreaties to join the trek of the Old Guard to Young Avenue. Moosie feels it would be like biting the Arm that raised her and, oddly enough, this loyalty has given her a reputation for savvy in the brewing trade. It was Moosie who suggested that Brucie's brewery build a full-scale replica of Josiah's last three-master, the *Rednose* (named, one can only assume, after the old dog's proboscis), and make it the corporate logo.

This choice turned out to be a superb public relations gambit, and the toast "Drink to the Foam" acquired a new meaning.* For her efforts Moosie was made Honorary Skipper of the Squadron, with her choice of colours (rust and puce), and Bruce was given the right to display three sheets to the wind. This union of sail and wassail seems to bear out old Josiah's dictum that the real wealth of Halifax has always depended on two things: "broors and hoors."

Actually, the closest Moosie ever came to resembling the latter was the year she became a painted woman in the Junior League's annual revue, "Knees, If You Please!" She was an absolute hoot, but the career of a Maritime Rockette soon palled, and she now gives her charitable all at the Kermesse Fair, a sort of High Anglican Hadassah.* Summers she plays pretty close to the Chester retreat, until Bruce pulls his jib and sails the family to the Island (Prince Edward) for the annual sojourn at Shaw's, with weekend forays to St. Pierre and Miquelon.

This annual pilgrimage re-enacts those dear dead days not quite beyond recall during the "Dry Twenties," when the Hedlund family imported as well as exported. Large consignments of extraterritorial high spirits were brought into Halifax under cover of Dartmouth, watered down to an acceptable level, and then relayed by the first unofficial U.S.–Canada pipeline to the waiting throats of the Americans.

All this go-with-the-flow was but a trickle compared with the recent increase in the firm's liquidity Stateside. It all started in West Palm Beach where Moosie, a non-beer drinker herself, had occasion to take a nip of Yank home brew after two driving sets of

---

*"Drink till yuh Foam" sez the wife, who is strickly W.C. to You.

*We has the same thing in Parry Sound. It's called yer Monster Sale and wives is tole to bring their husbins, and anything elts that's no more use.

tennis. "Not nearly as strong as I thought," she said between sips. "Rather like an off-batch of Sussex ginger ale."*

The next weekend, Moosie Hedlund presented her own case before Palm Beach society, and the rest, as the marketing men say, is hysterical. Moose brand has become the beer that made Milwaukee less famous.

Husband Brucie had been dabbling in Sable Island oil for years, but so far the only sable dividend his wife can call her own is that slightly dog-eared wraparound she inherited from her mother-in-law, with the same beady eyes and vicious claws. Right now she is too busy in her sou'wester supervising construction of *Rednose II* down in Lunenburg to worry about Brucie's dry holes. As tiny Moosie walks the planks of the latest replica of Josiah Dawes's prow, she will be clothed very like her noble ancestor in his last days, in a simple black gown and pearls, keeping alive the memory of the tall ships, and of the little women—behind the tall men—who made it all possible.

---

*The Dum Perrynon of ginjy ales, acorn to most Marmtiders.

Noo Brunsick

Noo Brunsick is the most underraped part of this country, and that's jist the way ther inhibitants seems to want it. They don't want the rest of us to noe how nice it reely is. That's why they have all them funny names fer places, like Buckteesh and Peenobskwish and Shiddyact. They want you to steer away from them, all you strangers, and leave them alone in their Parrydice. I thot all them names was old Injun till I tock to peeple in yer Sinjon River Valley (they'll talk back to me, cuz the wife is part herrin-choker and part bluenozer, sort of a herringnoser or a bloochoker), and I found out that them silly names are mostly Irish, frum that little Saint Brennan hoo cum over here in his little round bottom of a boat long afore yer Vikings with the horny hats. I dunno exackly wat spearit he was fill with wen he landed back in yer ate senchury but he wernt too steady on his see legs, wen he landed summers neer Beersvill. He made his way past Pettycoatyact, gittin unsted-dier all the time, takin time out to talk to the locals at Nash waak, Sis? and finely comin to rest at Napadogan. North of that is yer Mad Waskans and yer Acajun. I allus thot a Acajun was a small compack car till I met a bunch of them. They was doin the story of Evangeline, witch the wife and former sweethart wood of loved to have seen on account a that's wher she buys all her pantyhose.

But I'm digesting away frum ritch peeples, and in Noo Brunsick they is mostly absentease landlards livin off yer off iland like Nasso in yer Bananas. Noo Brunsick is sort of a republic gone a bit banana becuz of it. They got millyumairs hoo wood luv to settle down here, but they don't want to pay no incum tax, wich is why they outgo so much. Mind you, there's sum newritches up by Florence-ville hoo sticks around, and is bizzy cornerin the markets all over the world on a Glowball scale. But most uppity Noo Brunsickers is too blame well-bread fer to care much about makin money. They have long ago resine therselves to livin in a place that is a pon in the pam of sum malted millyumairs hoo has got more munny in ther pocket than the hole blame province has in its coffers up to Fredricktun.

"Brig" Hosmer made her fortune by listening to the men trade tips.

Gracious! Living in New Brunswick? Most of us Upper Canadians find this hard to imagine. But there is "Brig" Hosmer (*née* Margaret Trimmingham) happily splitting the difference between Fredericton and Bermuda, with the occasional fling on the French Riviera. Twice widowed, and looking for a thrice, she is undoubtedly the crazy glue that keeps this province together, despite what you may have heard about the power grid of citizens McCain and Irving dividing this feudal barony between them. It's really her Ladysir who controls both the fish and the chips of this province's net-dragging and gross lumbering operations.

I'll explain the bisexuality of Ladysir's official title later. The nickname "Brig" comes from her family's military background, starting with the forefather who was a conscientious objector during the American War of Separation. By 1783 her ancestor was forced out of his colonial status by George Washington's armed terrorists. Briggy is fiercely proud of claiming direct descent from one of America's first draft dodgers (they call themselves Loyalists now), and his great-great-great-granddaughter is still in command of the Tweedside D.E.A.F. (Daughters of Exported American Forefathers) Post.

Why did Brig's forefather choose New Brunswick instead of, say, the lush orchards of Niagara? The old artful dodger was the concert-master of the Pitt Orchestra in the burg of the same name, and he heard that N.B. was a good place for fiddleheads. Alas, the only provincial culture at the time was growing wild and untended, and the only Canada Council grant to be had was a hundred acres of uneven soil near Saint John, which is still noted for its ups and downs.

If Brig's pacifist fore-pa had been in uniform, he would have qualified for a thousand acres. The Trimmingham family has been warlike ever since. The next generation ignored the pleas of their non-combatant fiddler on the hoof and donned the uniform of the Quis Pam Sis Fusiliers. (Try that on the twist of your tongue three times rapidly in polite company.)

Eventually the Hosmer brigade pitched camp with all its followers in Gagetown, named after the peculiar roots the Passamaquoddy Indians used to smoke as a token of peace, or something like that. Briggy was born an army brat, but spent her adolescent life off-base at Peckerwood School for Girls, where she won the nickname Brig, partly by being the daughter of a brigadier, but mostly because she spent so much time in preventive detention. After graduation, she chose not to go on to higher ed. at Mount A. because although the Trimminghams were "Old Family," they were also "No Money."

Brig took a secretarial course in the Boston States instead, ended up touch-typed and short-handed, and got a borderline job in St. Stephen because her parents were chockablock with the Ganong throng. It was there she met Billy Aiken,* the Boy Plunger, who at the tender age of seventeen did amazing things with other people's money. Most Ganongites had had quite enough of Billy Aiken to last them a lifetime, but dear little Briggy had her desk pressed close to the wall of the men's lav, and she couldn't help overhearing the up-and-coming teen-age tycoon dispensing his stock tips. Brig banked on all of Billy's hunches and managed to salt away quite a few blue chips.

It was her heart, not her head, that led her to work for Bradstreet Dun at a time when his creditors were pounding on his door, threatening to make Brad live up to his surname. His lovestruck secretary offered to bail him out, and she had the million in Aiken investments to back her claim. Brad went down on one knee, proposed, and disposed of Brig's swag in one and the same gesture. From then on, Briggy made all the investments in the marital partnership, and they had their fortune made while K.C. Irving was still a pump jockey. Unfortunately Brad's own pump stopped working when it was blocked by a clumsy clot, and he infarcted himself to extinction.

One of the pallbearers was Burpee Hosmer, whose family had gone to seed in the bush to make their fortune. After a decent interval of bereavement, Burpee carried Brig off to Fredericton,

---

*Later becum Lord Beeverbored as soon as he reeched his peer age.

where she has since become the uncrowned queen of Waterloo Row. (Everyone on that distinguished thoroughfare, I feel sure, would love to crown her.) It was her continuing financial acumen that resulted in Burpee's knighthood: he was honoured for having more money than the province he inhabited.

Having lumbered his way to wealth, he later fell into dredging and became pretty well fixed in reinforced concrete. Briggy herself enjoys her own bridge work and has managed to throw several across the river, while holding onto her own private line (N.B. Tel, fifty-one per cent). Both Brig and Burp have been extremely generous with their well-gotten gains, which is why their province looks so well endowed.

Widowed again when Burpee fell off a wagon during a visit to Drydock Sanitarium,* Briggy now insists on being called Ladysir Hosmer, keeping her promise that she will keep Burpee's name forever—he never said which one—while she discreetly shops around for a new surname.

And why not? She is the proud owner of a white frame set well back in a charming Cape Cod style that is reminiscent of early Howard Johnson's. Her prominent bay window overlooks the St. John River valley, one of her first wedding presents from dear Burpee (the valley, not the window). "I feel the whole province is my dowry," she muses dreamily, as she stands below a personally autographed oil portrait of King George (the III, of course) and drums her fingertips on a genuine Sheraton table, wrested from the hotel chain of the same name by Burpee Jr. after a football weekend in Antigonish.

But she is proudest of all of the plague on her house. Oops, sorry, that should have been *plaque*. It states modestly, "Benedict Arnold Slept Here."* The frame house next door is occupied by another controversial figure, Premier Richard Hatfield. Brig says the only plaque he can claim is on his teeth.

---

*A home fer yer Alkyholics Unanimuss.
*A hy-rank Yank hoo defected over to our side.

Cuebec

*I*f ther is one place in this country I feel non-quallyfried fer to speek on, its yer province of Cuebeck. All I noe is that yer 1980 referee-endum sed that they dint want to separate from Canda, and all they bin doin is splitting ever since. Yer Angledfone munny keeps splittin to Tronto, and yer Frenchfone munny keeps gittin invest in Florider, so that the place is startin to be call Cuebec Sued.

Wat sprises me is that ther is still a lotta high mucky-muck WASCS (White Anti-Saxin Celts) left in Cuebeck. Speekin histercly, it was yer Scotch and yer French that uncovered this country wile lookin fer free beevers coast to coast. Summa them intermarry with eech other, wile the rest got matey with yer injun. But ther's Cuebeckers today with Scotch names cant speek a worda English. (Most English thinks that's troo of most Scots ennyways.) You take that Raw Bare Burns hoo was in Reamy Leveckyou's first cabinet, his natif tung was pure Garlic.

Every yeer them Kelts git in their Kilts and have a ringtail snorter of a Kaley (witch is Kiltic fer a party), and yuh won't see a pair a pants the hole nite. They git all dun up with ther sporms well hung in frunt, and start reeling around with sum yung debyoutramp. And the dansers is oney aloud to drink water wile

60

they're out there shakin a boot. Funny kind of Scotsmen but the wife says they're morn likely Pressedbyterrians. They jig therself and strathspay and hornypipe all nite. They bin doin this fer a hunnert and fifty yeer, and the munny that's raze is sposed to go to yer Sin Androo Sassiety to take care of poor immigerunt Hi-landers hoo bin livin the lowlife over heer. Wisht the wife and I cood quallyfy but we was brung up in Uppity Canda.

Up, up and away with Mazolair.

*I*magine me, Valerie Rosedale, higher than a kite, night-riding in a biplane built for two! Beside me, my charming hostess, pilot, and navigator, Mazo Laroque-Fortier, Madame la Présidente and sole shareholder of Mazolair, Mazomines, and Laroque Pétroléum. Below us, the bright lights of Mazolaville and Roque-Fortier twinkle like stars. Mazo is mistress of all she surveys—and, knowing Mazie, she probably did the surveying herself!

We first met on the playing field at Miss Edgar's and Miss Cramp's School, where she stick-handled more balls into Splits Puddock's goal mouth than all the other forwards' passes put together. The goalie cried foul, but Mazie claims that her uncanny ability to slip in between Splits's padded thighs was due more to comic asides than to illegal off-sides.

Although she didn't speak a word of English when she first came to the school,* by the time she had finished, Mazo could talk rings around us Anglos in both languages. We learned more about French letters from Mazie in the dorm after lights out than we ever picked up in the classroom. Some of her tips on the French tongue were a bit twisted, though. "Thanks to me, Splits still thinks French letters are weather balloons from the St. Pierre and Miquelon Meteorological Office!" Mazo chuckles with Gallic *élan*.

She could never understand why we found it so hard to pronounce our *Ps et Qs*, when French is such a frank, logical language, while English is a semantic *mélange*. Splits took this to be an anti-semantic remark and retorted: "What good are French Pays and Queues? The pay's too low, and the queue's too long."

Mazo maintains that her family owes its fortune to anti-French prejudice. Her forefathers and mothers had homesteaded in Mani-

---

*Yer Edgars and yer Cramps. (I never had a case of Edgars meself.)

toba's Red River Valley, until the government surveyors came along and plotted only for the English. Starting from scratch up the Saskatchewan River, Pierre Laroque supplemented the meagre family allotment by teaching school to a dozen local kids, all of them his own. In 1890 the Manitoba government abolished French-language education, and Grandpère Laroque was out of a job. This was *la paille ultime*, the last straw. They packed everything onto two wagons and headed east for the wilds of Ontario. They settled in a French settlement north of Sudbury, hard by Cobalt, as they say up there.

Hard indeed, until 1903, when railroad crews uncovered some lunar-looking rocks with silver veins. Before you knew it, the whole of Northern Ontario was off ore-hunting. Grandpapa Pierre thought his neighbours had rocks in their heads, but Grandmère thought she'd seen some chunks just like them in her vegetable garden. By combining some prospecting with her spring planting, Grandmère managed to strike a vein right under the turnip patch.

The mine had been yielding half a million dollars' worth of silver a month for several years by 1912, when the Ontario government passed Regulation 17, abolishing French in Ontario schools. This put Grandpapa in a towering rage, but Grandmaman took it as a sign from Heaven to head east once more, in search of brighter prospecting. They moved over to the Quebec side of Lake (for *lac* of a better term) Timiskaming, as soon as their palatial new "cottage" could be completed. I always thought its name, "Chalet Huit Dansent," came from *The King and I*, but Mazo tells me that it refers to family celebrations following the happy exodus of Mater, Pater, and the six littlest Laroques.

By then the horseless carriage was swinging into mass production, and automobiles became Grandpère's passion. In those days it required every ounce of human ingenuity just to keep the things moving at all. Weekends and holidays from spring thaw to first frost, the clan would head off on touring expeditions. During the frequent pauses for mechanical adjustment, the three boys did most of the actual work while Grandpapa Pierre hunted through the tool-box. His language on these occasions being unsuitable for young ladies' ears, Grandmaman would march the three girls off with shovel and pick to do a bit of hunting and pecking in the surrounding hills. Spare-time prospecting has been an extremely profitable family tradition that Mazo proudly maintains to this day.

"J'aime souvenirs" is Quebec's motto, says Mazo.

She is frequently to be seen in her favourite bonnet leading a procession of grandchildren off into the hills beyond Val d'Or (no relation to yours truly!).

During the First World War, Quebec's resistance to conscription led to the cute slogan "A vote for Laurier is a vote for the Kaiser," and the province found itself shut out of power, while Borden's condensed coalition milked the country. As Grandmaman put it, "They stole my land, they cut off my tongue, and now they want my sons for cannon fodder!" Nevertheless, the French-Canadian contingent, the Vandoos,* was responsible for the only victory of the Somme offensive. After that, things got even more offensive, and when the Vandoos broke through the Hindenburg Line, in one of the Allies' most brilliant exploits, every single officer was lost, including Pierre *fils* (Junior, that is). The second son, Réjean, Mazo's *cher papa*, joined the Royal Flying Corps. The first batch of R.F.C.s had all been knocked out of commission, so by then half of the Corps was Canadian. They said they didn't normally take "Froggies," but as Réjean had been to Cambridge they supposed it was all right.

It might surprise you that such staunch defenders of French-language rights should have sent all of their children to English schools. It was the Laroques' firm conviction that if all Anglophone children went to French schools, and all Francophone children went to English schools, Canada could solve its identity crisis in no time. As Mazie puts it, "We must be at least half as smart as the Swiss, and they seem to be able to cope with four language groups in a country the size of Lake Ontario!"

Mazo's father came back a changed man. He'd won his wings, but his mother began to wonder if he was ever going to come down to earth. He became a bush pilot, flying all over the northern territory, which had never been mapped. Réjean must have touched down for more than refuelling, however, as he managed to marry his Mont Royal fiancée. Marie-Hélène Mercier was dumbfounded to find herself roughing it in the northern bush, when her new mate was supposed to be worth millions. According to Mazo's mother, if it hadn't been for enforced lay-overs, to overhaul the planes, her five children might never have been fathered at all. Back then they flew in open cockpits, and one time Papa Réjean came home with the

---

*That's yer Garlic meenin' sweet wine.

66

The Laroque-Fortier "Mazoleum."

hands frozen to the joystick, keeping him out of trouble for some time.

With Réjean under wraps, Marie worried about being stranded on the frozen tundra. She decided that if she was going to share her husband's lot, she'd better get her own hands on the joystick and go mobile all the way. She was even more surprised than her husband when she turned out to be a crack pilot. The Laroques became a team—one at the controls, and one keeping an eye on the ground for anything that glittered. By the time little Mazo was old enough to walk, she was just plane crazy like her parents. She and her four siblings became known as the flying "Laroquettes" for the aerial acrobatics they executed while delivering Eaton's catalogues north of the treeline. (Their mother thought it would be good training for the kids to have a paper route.)

Meanwhile, Grandpapa Pierre had passed on, leaving his empire in the hands of the remaining son, Mazo's Oncle Antoine. It seems Antoine was too busy getting other rocks off to mind his deposits. Despite Grandmère's valiant efforts, by the time the stock market crashed, all that remained of the Laroque mining business was the pits. It's a good thing Mazo's mother had spotted that uranium, or the Laroques' fortunes would have fallen on hard times. By the time the next "war to end all wars" came along, business was booming.

Mazo volunteered her services as an ambulance driver for the Red Cross, as girls weren't allowed to fly. While on active duty she met Théophile Fortier, a dashing bombardier. Although heir to the Quebec dry-goods emporium Fortier et Masson, Théo was a grease monkey at heart. He and a couple of bombardier buddies were stuck on the idea of making a motorbike on skis that could go *un-deux-trois*-skidoo all through the winter. For the first ten years of their union, Théo was up to his chassis in axle grease, too busy tinkering to bother with business.

A lot of girls would have washed their hands of the whole greasy affair, but Mazo decided to roll up her sleeves and pitch in. Oil seemed to be the best way to fuel the whole operation. Applying the base-metal instincts she'd inherited from her family, Mazo set her sights on cruder stuff. I hate to gush, but that girl's uncorked more bubbly than anyone I know.* Laroque Pétroléum made more

---

*Oil wells that end well, I allays sez.

than enough to get Théo's pet project into mass production. Bombardier Skidoodles have been selling like hot cakes ever since— or as Mazo has so quaintly phrased it, "They're going like a load of crêpes!"

Nowadays, Mazo has gone from liquid gold back to the real thing.* In five short years she has become one of Canada's biggest bullion producers, with pots of gold stockpiled in her vaults. Before she came along, the debt-ridden mine was about to cave in, but Mazo stepped in and trimmed all the fat off the operation, keeping her overhead low and her profit high. Her recently completed stately home, Château Laroque, dominates the landscape. Perched high on a hill, it overlooks the thriving communities of Mazolaville and Roque-Fortier. (Mazo says that's not true—she oversees everything, but never overlooks anything.)

Meanwhile, Théo has taken his cue from his bullion bride and gone underground. Still fooling around with everything that moves, he has most recently created a new subway train engine. I guess he must be on the right track, because the city of New York just ordered a whole fleet of them. Théo named his latest triumph "La Roquette," in honor of Mazo, the high-flying gal who managed to get him started, kept him going, and took him full steam into the core of the Big Apple.

---

*Pepsis prefers gold to Coke, I gess.

69

"Dodo" Orford and Sheik Yabooti go native in the middle Eastern Townships.

Dorothea "Dodo" Orford Yabooti

Dodo Orford is one of those Anglos,* some would say acute and others obtuse, who stomped out of Montreal soon after René Lévesque took Quebec in '76. Most of my West-mount bosom buds followed the Sunlife out of *la belle province* and headed straight for Toronto. Not our Dodo, who still refers to my home town as Cochonville. She says she did her time in T.O., thank you, when she was head girl at Loathsome Hall. As a Loathsome Old Girl myself, I can attest to the fact that she ran a tight dorm. I never saw anyone take so readily to absolute author-ity—not since the days of Genghis Khan. I'm sure Dodo would have liked to seize the reins of power and run the whole school herself, rather along the lines of Royal Military College or that other fine Kingston institution, Millhaven.

Pity Dot never married, never found the inmate with whom she could share and endure life's long stretch. For all her stiff upper lip, she was the most popular house guest on our social circuit because of her wondrous ways with our recalcitrant offspring.* Bags of fun with a sherry under her belt, she always brought order out of juvenile chaos with her sergeant-major's bark. But she never bit and never raised a finger, much less a hand, to any of the young rebels. They all adored her non-violent discipline and jokingly called her Anti Maim.

Marriage and a family would have suited Dodo perfectly because she never backed away from a good fight. Completely bi when it came to linguals, she always hoped to open a crackerjack Anglo-French finishing school for young ladies of both persuasions. But the P.Q. victory and Bill 101 quashed all that, so before one could say sovereignty-association she sold, for much less than cost, the ancestral homestead at 1295 Sherman-on-the-Mount.

---

*Another werd fer WASP (White Anty-Sexyall Protestant).
*We ornery folks calls them spiled brats.

Sound like the act of a cowardy custard? Not on your *vie, ma vieille*! Dodo lit out straight for the family cottage at North Hatley, the Anglo Riviera of the Eastern Townships. Why, Dodo's great-grandpapa, General Chickasaw Mountain Orford, practically founded the place. He was one of those losing generals in that not-so-Civil War between those uppity States. When the war ended, he broke his sword over Lee's knees and migrated to Canada to pick up the pieces. Coming to Canada was one way of getting around all those "damyankees," and he liked the sound of the new word he heard, "Confederation." He figured these people might accept all the funny money he got for selling out the plantation way down upon the swampy river. He tried to sell off his slaves, too, but they reminded him that that was what the war had been all about.

The General headed first for Richmond, Quebec, and was relieved to find that General Grant had not taken it. But he longed for a bucolic existence and started his own Reconstruction period on the shores of Lake Memphramagog, and later on Lake Massawippi (Chickasaw liked to call it Lake "Massah, whip me," to recall happier days when he could hear slaves singing on the old plantation). Grandpapa started a cottage industry in this district that is still thriving today. Most of them still have that Southern ante-bellum look. The Hovering Manor, named for its plenitude of grovelling menials, maintains all the traditions of the old South and looks for all the world like Tara in its boom d-ays. The Cull House, the epitome of Southern North Hatley hospitality, is heady with the ambience of early Tennessee Williams and evokes an atmosphere of crawling wisteria, though none of the original Cull girls is left.

Guess who was the first person Dodo ran into when she booked into the Hatley Inn for a couple of days while the workmen removed the storm doors on her cottage? None other than René Lévesque, dropping ashes all over the Axminsters! He had holed up at l'Auberge Hatley (oh yes, he had already changed the name) with his cronies to choose his first cabinet. As I recall, the lovely old place has a good selection of well-crafted antique pieces from which to choose, or shoplift, in the case of one member of the P.Q. who didn't mind his.

While she was at the Auberge, Dodo sent me a postcard view of Mount Orford (the only high rise in the vicinity), with an invitation on the back to come social climbing any time. After that initial postcard...zip. Had Dode forgotten my code? I decided to forgo my annual June pilgrimage to Ogilvy's with tea after at that heavenly hostelry on Sherbrooke Street. Putting off the Ritz, I floatplaned direct from our local island airstrip across from the yacht club and landed smack in front of Chez Orford-sur-le-lac. The cottage was bolted tighter than my hubby on New Year's, and it appeared that Dodo had done the same. All this at the height of the season, which at North Hatley is five o'clock every afternoon, with compulsory attendance at all cocktail parties in the immediate area.

But this was merely lunch-time, so I bombed over to the Hob Nob, the gathering place for gourmands. It too was boarded up. There was one centre of information left for news, dirt, and gossip: the benches beside the North Hatley Club tennis courts. Here is the seat of leisurely, philosophical discussion, largely due to the interminable wait for one of the four tennis courts. I plunked myself down beside a blueblood in whites and asked about Dodo's whereabouts. He fixed me with a fishy stare and was about to answer when there came a cry from the courts. A heart attack close to the net had made one of them suddenly available. Racquets filled the air, cleared the fence, and clattered on the court, asserting their owners' territorial imperatives. My blueblood non-informant leapt from his bench as soon as he had thrown his Prince over, and I left in the middle of a fierce four-way fight for possession.

I finally got the Dodo lowdown between bites of a *croissant* * from the *séparatiste* who runs buns to all the "strange summer ones." Across the road from her *boulangerie* was a boarded-up gas station. It was there the event happened that changed the face of North Hatley, perhaps forever. Dodo was self-servicing her Porsche at one of the pumps when a fifty-foot stretch Mercedes drove up, disgorging an Arab sheik and seven veiled ladies. The sheik seemed to know nothing about servicing himself, and the ladies in harem pants were shifting restlessly from one curly-toed slipper to the other—potty time, obviously. Without a word, ex-Loathsome head girl Dodo took charge. She put the proper nozzle in the sheik's hand and unscrewed the cap so that he could fill his tank, then marched the seven veils straight to the station washroom to drain theirs.

---

*A kinda Frenchy hot cross bun.

From that moment on Dodo Orford became indispensable to Sheik Suleiman Yabooti of the Emirate of Baathtoof. He was visiting North America with a few of his wives in order to find out what had happened to the oil shortage. The people of North Hatley suspect that he was trying to create one, since he bought all five gas stations in the area and immediately boarded them up.

Everywhere the sheik went, Dodo was not far behind, acting as business adviser and lady-sitter, a eunuch position, I would think. Dodo threw a cocktail party at the cottage and Sheik Yabooti was the guest of honour. He brought along several six-packs of Dom Pérignon for the guests and a case of Bullshead ginger ale for himself,* and proceeded to announce his plan for the reconstruction of the area. There was to be a Space Research Centre, and to that end he purchased, on the spot, an abandoned drive-in theatre. He also wanted to install rocket satellite launchers and turn the area into a nuclear non-freeze zone. The sheik's military bent rather upset some of the intellectual novelists and poets who hang around the social fringe of North Hatley's upper crust, cadging free booze.

To divert attention, Dodo arranged for him to buy the hardware store, plus the local Dairy Queen to take care of the software. He wanted to take the summer theatre, the Piggery, and turn it into a disco called the Sheepery, and he also had plans afoot to purchase either Hovey Manor or the Hatley Inn and change the name to the Ramadan Inn. So far both these establishments remain in infidel hands.

So, apparently, does Dodo. One night the sheik folded his money and silently stole away. His mosque at Sunni Acres is boarded up, along with the Hob Nob, the hardware, the Dairy Queen, and the five gas stations. The most serious complaint voiced by the locals so far is that they have to travel at least eight miles now to get tanked up.

The mystery of Dodo's whereabouts was cleared up last week when I got an airmail from her with lots of wiggly squiggles on the postmark. It was written just after Dodo's Gulf honeymoon in Abu Dhabi to announce that she has taken the veil, but true to form, she is giving orders rather than taking them. Our own Loathsome head girl is in complete charge of the sheik's other eighty-six wives, and from her letter I gather that she runs a pretty tight harem, just like

---

*Yer Muslin is tea-total, and drinks cawfee that tastes like ground-up cigars.

the dorm back at our old *alma mater*. I get the impression that Dodo rules not only the roost, but also its rooster. Her plans for a finishing school in North Hatley to teach Anglo manners to young Francophone *mamzelles* are indefinitely postponed, because at this stage of her life, our darling Dodo Orford Yabooti has finally realized her fondest ambition. She is, without any doubt, the head mistress.

"We never buy off the rack, Val; even our sunsets are designer made."

Ontarryo

*r*uh noe wat's rong with ritch peeple? They ain't hungry.
And that's why us Canajuns can't compeet with yer Thurd
of yer Wurld that is, and is gittin ahead of us all the time.
You take them Queens Porkers in charge of us in this province.
Them fellas is like my bedrid Ant Perl, they ain't bin outa yer
House in morn farty yeer. Biggest thing on Billy Davis's ajender is
yer Doom Stayjum, now that we got a Freedom from Information
Act. (We alreddy got one, it's call yer Make Beleaf Gardens, and its
bin livin up to its name fer yeers wen it cums to gittin in yer
Stanleys Cups.)

But our lokel plutocraps is just as smug as a bug in a rug wen it
cums to yer futures. They awreddy maid ther piles, so they kin
afford to sit back on ther assets. They don't wanta noe about fifty-
generation computers (my gol, if I cood git a job in town wile I staid
livin in the country, I cood be an everyday computer). Even my boy
Orville who cant add or distract too good at school is intrusted in
going to a Floppy Dischotech, becuz he's bin playin with all them
viddlyo games like Packy Man and Honky's Dong. He sure don't
wanta be a farmer which is a honour without profit in our own
country; insted he wants to work up yer Sillycone Valley. His

mother thinks that's wher all the girls on "Hee Haw" comes from, but then Valeda thinks a transistor is a nun that has underwent a sex change. I tell Orville to git his electratonic trainin now before he is replaced by a roe bote. I don't meen one of them sitdown punts with two ores on the sides. I'm talkin about one of them tin men with chips fer brains and speeded-up mammarys like Arsy Dee Too or See Thru Peepio in yer *Star Wores* pitchers. Lee Iyacockeye claims that they help him with yer secund coming of Chrysler. But our capittlists better reelize soon that if Canda can't compeet with yer Thurd Wurld today, tomorrow we'll *be* yer Thurd Wurld!

Toronto's most prominent bag ladies, the Simp sisters.

I can think of no other part of the world, with the possible exception of Sicily, where a few families so completely dominate the financial infrastructure as they do in Ontario, the very nerve centre of the Canadian Establishment. As my Scots godfather used to say as he pointed me towards a stray coin on the street: "Infra penny, infra structure!" Cosy nostrums aside, this province has always been run on the Family plan, a well-bred mare's nest of interlocking relationships, perpetuated by a series of intermarriages that would make a Hapsburg's blood congeal in jealousy.

The first families of Ontario were either Huron or Algonquin, but the province was officially opened in 1784 in a ribbon-cutting ceremony in the vicinity of Yonge and Queen streets by the first Lieutenant-Governess, Lady SimpCo. (The Co. consisted of her three lap-dogs, Tiny, Tay, and hubby John, grave in braid and cocked hat.) Lady Simp was interested in trade rather than braid, and two centuries later the Simp Centre remains the focal point of Toronto's vagrant society, still *the* place for Canada's huddled masses to lounge, shop, and lift their eyes upward to catch a high-flying Snow goose.

The first SimpCo general store sold neither spirits, tobacco, nor playing cards. It opened late and closed early, and became an instant success with the good Torontonians. Soon a chain of such inconvenience stores spread across the country; the more remote areas were served by the SimpCo catalogue, a prime hang-up back then among northern residents who lived without the bare necessities among the hills and ravines of Rosedale.

The demise of her colonel did not deter Her Ladysimp beyond the mandatory half-day closing. He had been on half-pay since his retirement from the Armed Forces anyway. She simply had his body bronzed and placed inside the front doors of the shop with his last request to her emblazoned at the base of the statue: "Kiss My Foot!" A more permanent memorial was later erected in the form of St. John and All Simps United, a church built to the everlasting glory of All Simps, in loving memory of God.

The current retail operation (the store, not the church) is run by the descendants of Lady Simp, a quartet of merchant princesses, Daphne (Dibs), Melissa (Pug), Mary Alice (Doonie), and Philippa (Biffy). However, these are not the names they use in public. As modern merchandisers in a male-ordered world, they realize the wisdom of transvesting themselves of their Christian names, and they sign the payroll as Fred, Jim, Tim, and Wotan.

Wotan, named after the Nordic god of take-overs in the hopes that the baby of the litter would take some interest in the family business, has confounded all hopes by becoming the outdoor sport. She is content to search for the Amazon's mouth on a wind-surfer, break the sound barrier with her stereo recorder, or sponsor the Ralph Lauren Ladies' Polo Meet. Fred runs the Simp Centre by remote control from her King City country estate, Brae King Wyndes. Jim managed the catalogue division as a cottage industry from the baronial castle in Muskoka (which uses Lake Rosseau as its moat) until the annual publication, unfortunately, had to be cancelled when cottagers turned it into a one-page rip-off. The real disappointment has been Tim. Originally designated as trimmer and pruner of the various branches of the Simp family tree, she has become an undercover union organizer and is attempting to take over the operation by furtive thrusts from below.

Fortunately the blonde sheep of the family, Wotan, has come back into the family's good graces by her marriage to the Blatta boy. The Blatta saga is a heart-warming success story that makes Cinderella sound like a shoe-in. Hamish Blatta was a blacksmith in the Hebrides who hot-footed it over here after World War I to have a shod at the New World. He had the good Celtic sense to link up maritally with Ingrid von Boor, whose family controlled the exclusive Arty Shoppe, de Boors, in downtown Liechtenstein.

Together these two immigrants made a deal with Stanley Cann Paquers to take the skin off the backs of his meat products, and now their Clydesdale-type clodhoppers are worn by peasants in four-score countries. The Simp girl and the Blatta boy had known each other since they had done a dog and pony show at the Oakville

Gymkhana, on the Blatta estate in Blattawa.* Over the hill and cheek by jowl (give or take a few acres of landscaping) is High-brough Acres, owned by the slag king Al Fresco, whose fortune was built from a single nickel deposit. (Now that's what I call accumulated interest.) Al has been married several times, and his latest acquisition is Winnie de Poole, ex of Seth Poole, the present chairman of the Royal (not the hotel, or the bank, but the Winter Fair). Seth is son-in-law to Baskin Pissey of Put-on Broadcasting, who only attends affairs like the Royal and the Plate (the Queen's, of course) as a business obligation, since he's all tied up in cable twenty-four hours a day. The Old Bask is far prouder of his granddaughter, young golden Olsen, who is one of the top ten ranked snooker players today and is clearing tables all over the world. "I always knew the little shark would make it," he gloats.

A study of the mating habits of current Ontario tribes provides a key to the power grid they have so successfully maintained. The young are brought together at a pre-pubic stage, in nursery schools, gymkhanas, regattas, and birthday parties, then completely segregated by means of private schools and summer camps. The girls' camps are even more spartan than the boys'. Camp Onandonadog for young ladies on Lake Pipicaca is a survival course that prepares prospective Old Girls for any eventuality.

Of course, the eventuality they are really preparing for is marriage. The mating season usually begins in earnest at the weddings of one's best chums. Ushers and bridesmaids are paired off in carefully selected twosomes, and the success of such planning is demonstrated by the fact that the couple often end up at the altar the following year. The theory is that most young men need time to tire of anorexic models and overblown cocktail waitresses, and when they have, they will eventually settle down with a good sport who seems to be an awfully sound proposition and have a good head to boot. Likewise, most girls are simply looking for their fathers. It's better to fall deeply in like than head over heels in passion, their mothers reason. In this way, the continuity of the species, *homo estab* *establiens*, is assured.

I should point out that there is an exception that proves this rule. The glaring example that comes to mind is Lord Basserd of Front, the Marquis of Millhaven. At a time when distinguished Canadians

*Near Blattford, this side of Blampton.

Snooker queen the young golden Olsen likes to blow a big one before every shot.

are not allowed to go down on one knee to receive the flat of a sword on the pad of their shoulder for even a single knight, he has managed to gain access to the most exclusive House in the realm.

Born plain (and I mean this literally) Lloyd Basserd, in the Northern Ontario community of Nopusskissing, this brigand went from abject poverty to abject riches with alarming speed. His father was a wheel-tapper for the CNR until he was fit to be tied, but his son determined at an early age to be a mover and shaker in this country. Accordingly, his father retired, pulled him out of school at the age of fourteen, and got him a job on a construction site with a mechanical shovel. But making the earth move five days a week didn't satisfy the young Basserd. In his spare time he sat alone in his basement hovel playing with a pair of cat's whiskers. (There is no record of what he did to the pair of cats.) By rubbing the whiskers the right way he succeeded in receiving radio signals transmitted several hundred yards from his home. Taught by his mother that to give is more blessed than to receive, he learned to reciprocate the messages he heard, and developed his own five-watt radio station that sent messages in code to customers of local bootleggers and patrons of other clandestine establishments.

This tiny nest-egg soon ballooned into a huge conglomerate of underground stations purveying furtive information across the half-vast province from Wawa to Hornepayne. To accommodate the deaf, Lloyd put his subliminal messages in a local newspaper, the Timmins *McNuggett*. Next day he bought a copy of the paper to check the text of his ad. The day after, he bought the whole paper, and he proceeded to buy a newspaper every day, from the executive suite on down to the printing presses and delivery vans.* When he was investigated by the government for running a combine (the employees thought of him as a bad-tempered thrashing machine), he was able to defend his radio stations in his newspapers and vice versa. "One hand whitewashes the other," he explained.

Back in 1952 commercial television was considered to be a licence to print money, but it was too slow for Lloyd, and CBC-TV had as strong a monopoly as the Royal Mint. It was impossible to do anything about the CBC (nobody ever has), but Basserd decided to give the mint a run for its money and put his printing presses on double time. Unfortunately the colour of his money was considered unacceptable by professional standards (the fifties weren't pink enough, the fives never true blue), and despite the finest lawyers and judges that money can buy, Lloyd was obliged to take a year's sabbatical near Kingston. His own newspapers from one end of the country to the other screamed the headline "LORD BASSERD OF FRONT!" It had been changed in the composing room by a nervous typographer who feared for his job and refused to print "LLOYD BASSERD AFFRONT!" Many think that it was from this moment that a confused public began to accept his jump from steerage to peerage. "The noblest peer of them all," proclaimed someone standing next to him in the prison washroom.

Lloyd brought many reforms to the penal system during his short stay, including the introduction of such social services as the Diner's Club card, to provide an efficient gourmet service with

---

*He went frum rags to ritches by printin all the rags.

imported wines and topless dancers. Oddly enough, it was during his stay in stir that he achieved his utmost mobility in financial markets. He started a travel agency inside his cell and managed to send fellow prisoners all over the world, where they became agents for new ventures in his name. Most important was his discovery and development of the huge Black Sea oil resources. "Why'd ya think it was called Black in the first place, dummy!" Lloyd crowed at his critics. What was the secret that made this man the most powerful absentee landlord in the world, especially while he was confined to 100 square feet of Canada as the guest of its government? The answer is, as always, a woman.

No one contests Lord Basserd's claim to Best of Breed in the chauvinist pigstakes. He wasn't nicknamed "No Broads in the Boardroom" Basserd for nothing. Everyone remembers his dictum to women's commentator Patsy Crump: "The only position you dames should ever take is flat on your backs!" After that he was re-nicknamed "All Broads on the Broadloom," but no one knows for sure how many employees he has called on the carpet. But the one fixed point in his life was the only human being with a more commanding voice than his own, his personal secretary and executive assistant, Dessa Bell Nickerson. He first met her in the Nickel Range Hotel in Sudbury (the price always appealed to Lloyd), and from that moment on Dessa went on the warpath until she marched Lloyd down the Bridle Path. This was 1933, the year in which Lloyd lost most of his money at bingo, but this didn't deter Dessa. When she saw the wolf at the door, she grabbed the opportunity to get her first fur coat.

Running her husband's affairs from their country estate in the Caledon Hills, Greed Acres, Dessa has also managed to develop her Lord's deeply submerged cultural side. At the same time as he bought a controlling interest in the office copier company Zerocks-off, Dessa found the equivalent in the world of painting. Cornelius Fleaglehoff was a nineteenth-century Russian émigré who painted the same picture many hundred times at the same time of day and from the same angle. The only differences were that the people and the animals moved around a bit. (Not much, mind you, it was winter.) But it was Dessa who taught her Lloyd and master the difference between an original Fleaglehoff and the copies that were hanging in banks and barbershops across the country. "Look, Lloyd, these ones with the hardware calendars on the bottom are

"I finally had to tell him, Val, that the real Fleaglehoff paintings are the ones without the calendars at the bottom."

copies," she instructed. Lloyd dutifully tore the months off and sold them in the thousands from door to door.

What does the Front in Lord Basserd's title refer to? Most people assume it is the money he put up to buy his title in the first place. His wife claims it refers to the corporation he carries before him wherever he goes. He himself refers to it as the location of Toronto's first domed stadium, donated by him to show those *parvenus*** in Vancouver and Calgary that they aren't the only ones capable of a big cover-up. The fact that Toronto already had Maple Leaf Gardens did not deter the Big Basserd in the slightest. He was determined to provide the city he has adopted (and paid for) with a first-class venue in which the finest artists could display their musical gifts. Dessa says that Lloyd's idea of the finest would be the pipe band of the Forty-eighth Highlanders following along behind the RCMP Musical Ride six nights a week all year round. Fortunately his wife took charge of the venture, and now Dessa Bell Hall is home to string quartets, opera singers, ballet dancers, and other high-class subsidized artistic hangers-on. The lowest attendance record so far was for the hearings of the Kept Commission investigating the Monopoly game played by Canadian newspaper publishers. Lloyd made the most of the occasion by displaying across the width of the great dome a banner that read: "Owners of the World Unite! We Have Everything to Lose! Our Chains!" Needless to say, the Kept commissionaires succeeded in pulling nobody's chain.

Oh dear, I suppose we should pay some attention to the *nouveaux riches*,* who are at present in danger of becoming the *nouveaux pauvres*.* So it's time they had their day in court (before they skip the country!). This new breed of entrepreneur is not so much interested in buying up companies as in selling out one another. Students of economic history are by now familiar with the decline and fall of the Greco-Roman Empire, but surely it bears repeating for those who may have missed this transient event. Transient seems to be *le mot juste** to describe the characters of Steve Greco and Arnie Roman, although they prefer to refer to themselves as the Grand Acquisitors.

---

*Garlic for Johnnies cum lately on the spot.

*Easy cums.

*Easy goers.

*Just a word.

"Val, you'll love Ontario: a place to status and a place to quo."

Steve Greco was brought up in a lumpen-middle-class family in London, Ontario, believing that the only way to lead the life of Riley was to sell insurance. He was given the task of selling tornado insurance in Oxford and Lambton counties. No takers. So the company, Mutual of Palmerston, let him have a shot at the life-term division. Greco took one look at the actuarial tables and figured out from the highway statistics that an even quicker turnover on the road to a fast buck was selling used cars. He rented a swamp, threw in some duckboards leading to the public phone booth that was to be his office, and borrowed some stolen cars. He realized that London was a WASP-dominated area and that he needed a less ethnic name than Greco to draw trade. He picked up a flag from a high school production of *Pirates of Penzance*, flew the skull and cross-bones proudly, and called himself Jolly Roger: "Every deal a steal, come in and walk the plank!" was his slogan. He moved a million five in three months. His business rivals still refer to him as "Hell" Greco.

Always looking for bigger and brighter horizons, he next became convinced that there was more money in the crankcase than in the car, and threw his profits into offshore oil. Having put his money into energy, he then put his energy into selling sex through soccer. Convinced that women would go wild about strapping young men in silken shorts with no extra padding, he persuaded high-fashion model and star ballet dancer Duane Glitzy to apply his fancy *entrechats* to waltzing rings around a soccer field. Unfortunately nobody else seemed to be in the same league, and the fans stayed away in droves.

At the same time as this was going on, Arnie Roman was forty miles away flipping hamburgers in a greasy spoon in the little village of Dumbo, named after P. T. Barnum's famous elephant, who got tracked down there in 1881 when he was too stupid to come in out of the train. The town hadn't had much excitement since, until young Arnie Roman started flipping companies as fast as hamburgers. A devout jogger to and from work, eight miles a day, he found it no sweat to be Johnny-on-the-spot, and whenever a cheap piece of property came into view, Arnie would buy it with a non-existent bank account, make a couple of phone calls while running on the spot, and have it sold at a profit before he got to his lowly steam table. He held on to one abandoned garage and grease pit and decided to start his own fast-food restaurant. "Roman's Meals...a Banquet fit for a Burgher!" This same sign now appears in forty-seven languages throughout most of the world. The chief exception seems to be the Soviet Union, which imposed a ban on meals that take less than three minutes, but Arnie's latest conquest is China, whose more than a billion people always feel hungry an hour later.

Eventually Greco and Roman made the same false move. They divested their prime assets when they dumped their first wives, the childhood sweethearts who had been with them through the lean and greasy years. These were replaced by "contract wives," willowy ex-cocktail waitresses who were assigned to hang on the Greco-Roman arms at business conventions and give them the up-to-date look of newly acquired affluence. But the real marriage of true minds was in the relationship between Steve and Arnie themselves. Together they planned to conquer the known world. Their determination was somewhat thwarted by a court decision that gave their ex-wives exactly fifty per cent of their ill-gotten gains. Worse followed.

The following summer Revenue Canada moved in and asked for their files. The audit people were referred to Steve and Arnie's mutual manicurist. Things have not gone well since the oil glut. "I told Arnie not to grease them hamburgers so much," wails Steve. Now both have given up jogging and are into out-of-the-body experiences, claiming that it saves on travel expenses. Their belief in extra-sensory perception has allowed them to cancel their answering services. Recently they purchased some Chinese junk without realizing it was some kind of boat. Right now, it's their best source of revenue, housing a floating crap game and bar called the Taiwan-on, three miles offshore of Nanaimo. I visited the former Mrs. Greco and Mrs. Roman, who live with their children in two London, Ontario, townhouses that vulgarly resemble parts of Caesar's Palace (the one at Las Vegas, not Herculaneum). "They're not bad slobs, really," said Connie Greco between blowing on her nails. "They just had no idea how they did all this. It wasn't their macho gall at all." "Nah," says Sandra Roman, "they was fine as long as we took care of business for them and let them play with their antique cars and yachts and jets. Little boys never really grows up, ya know. Their toys just get more expensive all the time." "Yeah," roars Connie. "Look what us cost them!"

Mannytobah

This place becum famous allover yer world and uther places on accounta the metrical sistern. Sumbuddy lode up one of them Dumbo jets on leeters thinkin they was galleons and the plane wasn't worth a continental wen it hadda cum bellyfloppin down haffway hard by Gimly, witch fer one breef nite becum the crotchrodes of yer world. But nobody has paid this province much mind ever since, sept mebby to boo Briney Bullroney or tell John Turner he was the gratest Tory ever sold. Mostly Canda defers to Mannytobah like it's not reely there, witch is a shame cuz wen it cums to alla crost Canda its one of my faverit open parts.

Winnypeg used to be our bredbin, but except fer them Richer Sons hoo is up to ther arrears in it, a lotta old ferms seem to have gon agin the grane and sold out. I notiss a lot more sellin out than buyin in with our home-groan millyumairs. They're sorta yer Cumpny of Old Canajuns gittin together everytime there's high intrust rapes and selling off their intrusts in Canda and movin frum Porridge and Main down to yer Carbean. Most home-groan munny is divested acrost yer boarder. Ritch peeples don't pay much mind to nashnul flags: the only principle-alities they saloot is places like Exxon and Zeerox.

That's why Mannytobah has turn out to be one big blanched plant. A lotta them jetsetters flies away so's they won't have to pay no taxes. I wish the pollytishuns wood reelize that it ain't tax cuts us poor peeples needs. We jist need to be garnteed that we will became rich, then we won't have to pay no taxes like them millyumairs.

a · mari · usque · ad · mare ·

Young "Commie" Brown: a real Red River Valley Girl.

How did a nice upper-class mid-Western girl earn the nickname "Commie"? Surely the result of a consonant mispronounced by a younger member of the family that became an inside joke. Not in the least! Even from the earliest days, all the girls at St. John's Ravenscourt referred to little Con as "Comrade Brown, baby Bolshevik." Her father, Montagu, heir to the Trim Reaper farm machinery fortune, got clubbed as a Red by our Redcoats during the Winnipeg General Strike back in 1919. Monty was simply attempting to enter the Manitoba Club on Broadway and didn't notice that he was being followed by more than three hundred red-flag-waving veterans ready to overthrow the Establishment.

Despite his protests that he was not protesting, Monty Brown was rounded up with the rest and incarcerated overnight. The blow with the billy must have knocked him silly, for he was not really right from that day on, but most decidedly Left. He emerged on bail the next morning a complete convert to the gospel of Karl Marx, Friedrich Engels, and Tim Buck, too. Fortunately there were no serious Reaper-cussions with the family bank account, and he was able to clip coupons for the rest of his days, as he raised his daughter on Regina Manifestos rather than Eaton Beauty dolls. At age eight young "Comrade" was picketing her family's plant ("Down with the Combines") while her father was trying to organize the U.G.G.*

Young Commie Brown came to realize the futility of power through politics by watching her father straining to learn conversational Icelandic as he tried for the Labor-Progressive seat in Gimli. He lost his deposit despite a desperate last-minute change of label to Conservative-Progressive. Two visits to the provincial legislature convinced Commie that her father had chosen the wrong route to

---

*Usual Grain Grousers.

power. "I sat under the Golden Boy," she confided, "and saw nothing worth a second look."

Trying to make the Red River Valley vote its true colour eventually palled on father Monty, and he ended his days as a religious mystic who always voted C.C.F.* By this time his daughter had reached her majority (fifty-one per cent of shares), and she began to yearn for exotic places. That was when Commie Brown moved to St. Boniface and spent seven years in voluntary exile, lapping up the culture and ramming the language down her throat. The result was a 700-page book that proved that Louis started the First Riel Rebellion in 1858 rather than 1869 and against his mother, not the government. The tome, *All Right, Louie, Drop the Gun*, now graces the remainder tables of bookstores across the country.

By now Commie Brown was a total apostate to her father's Leftism. She took a three week close-encounter group session with other millionaires at the CS Institute in Davos, Switzerland, and graduated *magna cum ego* in Creative Selfishness. Back home she prepared to enter the bull-and-bearpit of the Winnipeg Stock Exchange, but found herself plying her trade entirely on the phone, just like a racetrack tout.

In her absence the Trim Reaper and sixty-nine other companies had been swept up into the maw (or perhaps we should say the paw) of the Aggravus Corporation. This paper tiger had been unleashed by Barney McGougall on an unsuspecting economy in an attempt to relive his glory days on the Wartime Prices and Trade Board. "I got a dollar a year and earned every goddamn penny of it," Barney still boasts. But Barney got tired of waging peace against both government and consumer, and trundled off to Samoa. ("Samoa? How much do you want?" groaned his wife, Reg.) McGougall dragged his loot along with him, and Canada fell into its biggest post-war recession.

Comrade Brown had a look at the *real* annual Aggravus report, due to her majority status in Trim Reaper, and she decided she wanted the whole Aggravus business for herself. Titular control of this vast consortium had been entrusted to Barney McGougall's solicitors, Heehan and Sheehan and Meehan and Meehan, but a fight for actual control was brewing among the ageing lions in the compound.

*Not the bicycle cumpny, but yer erly socialites, now D.P.'s.

Commie's book tells the Riel Story about Louis.

To assist her in her one-woman take-over bid, Commie needed an accomplice as cool as herself. She found one in a Celtic Icelander in charge of the Xerox machine outside the chairman's office. When Comrade Brown and Blair Finbogassen set eyes on each other, it was love at first proxy fight. She wheedled a proposal out of him after the third chili dog at Kelekis's* Restaurant.

The Finbogassen-Brown nups were celebrated one Sunday on the floor of the Winnipeg Grain Exchange. Guests were limited to those mentioned in the Aggravus annual report. Invitations were sent out on Xeroxed copies of preferred shares, and even during the ceremony, trading was active, with more flutters than a short-circuited pacemaker. All the while the Dom flowed quietly like Bright's Catawba, and the bride and groom mingled with the crowd till all hours, exchanging autographs and signing loan agreements. By the time the bouquet was thrown, so were the majority of the shareholders. The happy couple, now completely in control, jetted off for a honeymoon at the Connaught.

The whole marital arrangement almost became null and void when Commie discovered that Blair had booked them into the Royal Suite of the Hamilton, Ontario, version of her favourite London hotel. However, love of power conquers all, and the extra-billing and cooing were curtailed as the delirious couple spent most of their time on the phone, dickering for control of Eldorado Smelting of Bethlehem, Pennsylvania. Their union was about to be blessed with a new stock issue, but paranoia overtook the Yank-dominated board, which feared a reversal of the 1776 irregularities. The young couple returned from Bethlehem with nothing to show for their pains.

After this disappointment the nuptial couple got down to the business of enjoying themselves. They borrowed money from Commie's Daddy (it's a wise child that owes its own father) and took the grand tour of the world (which takes a couple of hundred grand these days). They went to Europe for the season, subletting in succession Andorra, San Marino, and England. Hubby Blair went trout fishing while Commie went up to Champneys at Tring for a diet of raw veggies, cold crystal-clear tap water, and ultrasonic infrared suction cellulite treatments. Then on to Baden-Baden to

---

*Never herd the werd; it's Greek to me.

96

take the waters, he to fish, she to drink, and after dinner both of them to drink like fishes.

They returned to Winnipeg in time for the open season on Hungarian partridge and more hot dogs at Kelekis's, to allow the fatty triglyceride regime to begin all over again. The couple are hoping to create their own rustic English inn near Brandon, by throwing together several stone houses of the post-Riel period. All that one can ask after a hard day, they feel, is a hot bird and a cold bottle. Commie is giving in to her double chin; she feels that having only one is just too much work. Blair's idea for his next vacation is to stay home and let his mind wander. Commie's do-good father wants them to turn philanthropist, giving away publicly what his family had stolen privately, but visions of take-over bids are starting to dance in her head again. "It's the creative aspect of such plundering that intrigues me, not the money, Val," she confided to me over beer and gourmet pretzels. "After all, money isn't every-thing."

"I agree," echoed hubby Blair. "There's also stocks, bonds, travellers' cheques, and bank drafts."

"Such a tease," she giggled softly. "But my father has taught me that money can't buy happiness. Look at my old school chum, Berethea Brown-Cave-Mann; she has ninety million dollars. Do you think she is any happier than her school chum Pristine Garment, with only eighty million dollars?"

When I asked her what the greatest virtue in life was, she replied without hesitation: "Thrift. Especially in one's immediate ances-tors." What about the danger of the return of inflation? "The dollar can never fall as low as the things that some people will do to get one." Charity? "Must not be gone into for display purposes." Commie gives anonymously, refusing even to sign her correct name to the cheque. Usury? "My banker taught me one hard and firm rule. Never profit from the needy, because if you lend money to anyone who really needs it, you may not get it back."

A final question to this take-over daughter of a socialist dreamer: "Where will you make your next bid?" Commie Brown merely dimples and says, "Oh Val, it's hard not to think of the Bay."

Sass-cat-chew-on

ere's a pairaducks. The safest place in Canda durin the last depressed recessyun was the place that was hit hardest by yer deep depressyun in yer durty thurtys. Peeples that owns them big sexshunal farms out here will never be ritch as Creases, but they're dirtritch cumpair to the way they wuz dirtpoor in yer thurtys. Mind you, every time they has bumper-to-bumper crops of weet, the price gits bump down per bushill, so that they ends up makin morer less the same munny cum feest or famin.

Mind you, they still got them grassedhoppers around (wat the Bible calls yer low-cussed), and ther was a skeem fer to bring seegles out from Tronto fer to et them all up. Seegles ain't too poplar in Tronto after one of them got hit by sum Yanky-hankypanky baseball plair at the Exhibitionist's Park and now yer avridge Ontarioryan wants a big cover-up of a Dome Stayjum with a distractable roof. You'd think Sasskaktchewan was the place need a Dome over that Taylor Feeled, but Father Divine's guvmint sez no, so I gess Regina is gonna go on bein yer hemmeroid capitol of the world.

I think Saskytooners is still hurt about not getting their own teem of NH Hellers. The felluh put the kybo on that skeem was

Harld Ballhard, hoo sed the oney way yuh kin git to Saskytoon in winter time is by dogteem. Harld shood know, I spose, fer he's led a teem of dogs fer yeers.

Peagrim's Progress.

What a blend of two Great Spirits resounds in the names Barfman and Peagrim! Every day elbows are flexed the world over in tribute to this marital blend. But before the ethnic cocktail of the Barfman-Peagrim union was mixed, there is much to tell, my pets. *Fiddler on the Roof* has nothing on the fiddling and diddling that transpired in the southeast corner of Saskatchewan, in the shirtwaist years of this century.

Beancurd, Saskatchewan, was very likely the only community in the West named after the staple in its one and only restaurant, the Grate Wall (misspelling not mine, I assure you). Arriving in town on the Christian sabbath, Shlumke Barfman found Hoo Ling's Chinese restaurant the only Establishment open to him on that frigid Sunday in 1912. Courtesy of Sir Clifford Sifton, the Barfman family had been plucked from the pogroms of Royalist Russia to open up the Canadian West for us Eastern manufacturers.

Fresh from the steppes of the Czars, *paterfamilias* Shlumke, his wife, Golda, and their five children, Hersh, Pisch, Toosh, Abe, and baby Belle, settled temporarily on the back steps of Hoo Ling's Cantonese kitchen. "He tried to sell us egg foo yung," Belle reminisced to me recently after a few holes at the Sun Lakes Golf Course near Scottsdale, Arizona, "but *Mummele* felt the whole set-up wasn't too kosher." However, the Barfmans did accept an offer to rent Hoo Ling's outer house for fifty cents a month. That little shedhouse on the prairie is now preserved in bronze in the foyer of the Peagrim Building in New York and displayed as the cradle of a far-fetching global empire.

The dynasty-to-be started with a carriage trade in scrap wood, an exotic rarity in southern Saskatchewan in any era. While Shlumke and sons put their collective shoulders to the wheel (it was a horseless carriage), Momma Golda and little Belle put down roots in the Beancurd soil, in expectation of potatoes.

The wood trade was soon scrapped, but Hoo Ling had his eyes on the budding potato crop. His customers preferred chips and gravy to rice with their chops and suey. Trade relationships had scarcely blossomed between the inner and outer houses of Hoo Ling when the Oriental proprietor was suddenly forced to cash in his fortune cookies at the pearly gates. His sudden demise was the result of a Tong war with the adjoining establishment, Elsie's Beauty Salon.

It seemed that Dame Elsie and Hoo had a semi-detached relationship of their own. When Hoo Ling confessed that he already had a wife in another province (Hunan), Elsie dispatched her yellow pearl on the spot and headed off for foreign parts, address unknown. Hoo Ling's body was discovered by nine-year-old Belle soon after the heat of the moment. "I've got a feeling you're Hoo Ling," she mused, as she spied the charred corpse beside the now-cold curling irons.

The fact that there was no will left the way clear for the Barfmans to make their first take-over bid and absorb both establishments. When the winter's supply of potatoes froze solid, Momma Golda resorted to the time-honoured Slavic tradition of distilling their essence to liquid form, and in a short time Elsie's Salon doubled its second vowel. The inhabitants of Beancurd soon got wind of what was brewing. The joint establishment was renamed "The Belle Hotel," and from that day forward, the vat was on the fire.

The entire family toasted each other over a samovar of tea and sang, with the sugar between their teeth: "Barfmans never, never, never shall be Slavs." The advent of Prohibition in Saskatchewan in 1916 necessitated the construction on the saloon of a special side door with retractable slot, but also succeeded in tripling the family income. Belle was dispatched to the Little Flower Academy in Regina, to learn food chemistry and to major in Goyism, but she professes to remember very little about that Spanish painter.

It was the advent of the Volstead Act in the United States in 1920 that secured the family fortune for all time. According to Belle, the Canadian government's policy on illicit exports was "Speak easy and carry a soft *shtick*." Soon swarthy drivers in Duesenbergs, Armstrong Siddeleys, and McLaughlin-Buicks were running a regular take-out service across the forty-ninth parallel.

One of these furtive criss-crossers was Alastair Huish Peagrim, age twenty-three, the seventh son of the seventh son of the founder of a Scottish concern that had led its countrymen to buy distilled waters ever since Bonnie Prince Charlie was dragged away in Flora

MacDonald's unmentionables. With only a pittance of a remittance, Alastair was exported to Canada even before he had reached the age of maturity. He was sent to join the Barr colonists near Saskatoon, until it was discovered that they were devoted to Temperance.* Loafing his way through the Wheat Belt, young Peagrim ended up in Estevan as a burlap wrapper and spare driver for a group of North Dakota importers: Albert Capone, Salvatore "Three Fingers" Acapella, and Big Mackenzie "No Relation" Kingfish.

One day when Alastair made a pick-up stop in Beancurd en route to fulfilling his North Dakota quota, he spied our Belle squeezing the spirit from a sack of mealy potatoes. Their eyes met: he was rooted to the spot. She blushed and said shyly, "This spud's fer brew." It was love at first blight.

Alastair invited her outside for a peek at his Gray-Dort. Belle was intrigued, but when he suggested an evening out (to an undisclosed drop-off point near Fargo), big brother Hersh put the kibosh on it. Alastair was *tref*. Belle tells me this is a Yiddish word that means you couldn't have him at table. But Belle was smitten, even though father Shlumke threatened to tear her name out of the book.

"What book?" asked Belle, who had never seen one around the Barfman homestead.

"*Torah, Torah, Torah!*" thundered the patriarch.

The lovers were parted, but not forever, as the world well knows. Belle had a special kind of clout in the Barfman organization, despite her secondary sexual status. As the only non-drinking Barfman, it was she who decided whether the mash should be aged for one day or two. Belle went on tasting and spitting out the residue, and the pining Peagrim kept on drinking while driving, till Belle feared he might soon become her man of extinction. She took to sneaking out in the middle of the night and taking the wheel of his Gray-Dort herself. One night she was caught out by a bed check back home at the family hostelry in Beancurd. Momma Golda had a strict rule that all guests had to rise at six A.M. and return to their own rooms.

The rest of our story is *Financial Post*-history. Belle and Grimpy eloped, and for a time the Barfman products suffered a lapse

---

*Ther ranch was dry too. It was call yer Barr Nun.

103

Belle urges her reluctant poodles to use the moat.

in taste. This was a minor problem during Prohibition, when people would drink anything, but time always tells in the brewing industry. The Barfman-Peagrim merger was sanctioned by both sides upon repeal of the Volstead Act, when bathtub gin had acquired an all-too-familiar ring. Now the emphasis was on quality. Belle was brought back to spawn an empire that spans the globe and is even now reaching for outer space.*

What has been the secret of the Barfman billions? Most pundits point to Ma Belle herself, who is still cleaning up—and sometimes mopping up—after her brothers' disastrous handling of take-over bids. "Bids? *Bibs* they should have already!" roars Belle, with a rye grin.

According to Ma Belle, the creation of the irresistible "bouquet Barfman" was quite accidental. It seemed that the alkali-flavoured water of Saskatchewan, when combined with sulphuric acid, produced a slew of flavours that could not be matched anywhere. ("Just don't light a match to 'em," Belle warns.) At first, the tart taste on the tongue took a bit of getting used to. "Peagrim?" the customers would snort. "Ain't yuh got them two words backwards?" But Plum Royal, the premier product, continued, like

---

*I red the hedline jist reesuntly: "Canadian Distiller High on Moon Shuttle. Offers to Bend Arm."

Belle, to improve with age. It was originally called "Shivers Wriggle," and still remains wrapped in a mini-replica of its owner's purple flannelette nightie, in memory of that first furtive wedding night.

All that was thirty-five great-grandchildren ago. Most of the Barfman-Peagrim clan still gather for the annual Honky Festival (I hope I've got that right. It's their version of Christmas, at any rate) in Bellemoral Castle. The castle completely dominates the prairie landscape outside Estevan. Each morning, Belle stands beneath its flying buttresses and battlements, urging her poodles to use the moat. The variegated interiors are furnished in everything from Low Victorian to Art Nouveau glitz. Some of the pieces go back to Louis the Fourteenth. "I remember in '29," Belle reminisces fondly, "when most of our stuff had to go back to Eaton's the fifteenth!"

Dear Grimpy is gone now. He succumbed to a liver complaint during the Saskatchewan Seventy-fifth Anniversary Celebrations of 1980 and went to his final watering-hole. His widow says Grimpy's drinking problem was for lack of a seat in the Senate, while whipper-snappers like Beaverbrook, Bennett, and, worst of all, "Fleet of Foot" Thomson got titles.

Belle is now known locally as the Widow of *Hootspah*, an Indian word whose origin I can't seem to trace. To the world, of course, she will always be Ma Belle, but to family and friends she is just plain Booby. I thought this name referred to her ample figure, but she tells me it's a Yiddish title for grandmother, and she hopes to become a great-great-great-Booby many times over.

Another title she retains with pride is Honorary Colonel-in-Chief of the Peagrim Highlanders. She also keeps up her membership in the Beaver Club, given to the rare woman who has managed to spend six months of the year frigid in the West. You see, Belle reverses the usual pattern of the well-to-do Beaver. She winters in Saskatchewan and spends the sweltering summers in Arizona, a chip shot from the Sun Lakes Club.

Booby confesses that this perverse timetable is partly due to her one affliction (she jokingly refers to herself as "the girl from Emphysema"), gained from inhaling dangerous fumes in the line of duty. Whenever the bloom is off the latest batch of Peagrim Covert Reserve, a sample is shipped to Beancurd, Saskatchewan, immediately, for Belle is still the only Barfman with taste.

Elberta

Wat a topsytervy thing has happen to this place since Ock-
tober 28, 1980. Up to then Elberta was baskering in
posterity wile the rest of us in the country was bein pritty
well recessive. But out to Caligari the oney inflation problems was
gittin enuff overdraft fer their balloonin on their weak ends.

Alluva sudden, compleet arsy-versy. This was bout the time me
and a lotta other Easterners were thinkin of hitchin up our
stayshun waggins and heddin west. So wat happen on that fetal day
in October, 80? It were the berth pangs of yer Nashnul Elegy
Polissy brung up by Alien McKickin in his second bludget. Buyin
our country back frum yer Yank had bin on a lotta our minds since
Conflagellation, but at a time wen intrust rapes was sky-hy this
seemed too much and too late. Yer oily shortedge had got a sudden
attack of yer gluts. Peter Luffhed's guvmint thot of their province
as a one-crop economee now that them Arbs had us over a barl. We
spent all our search munny on yer Tarpits and up yer Blowfort See.

Wot coz yer glut that kick Elberta in the gut? Well, it was jist us
little peeple cuttin down on our consumptivness. But Elbertans say
it was that Nashnul Elegy Pogrom that made all the big rigs to stop
ther drills and hed back over yer forty-nine parrlells of lassitude like
they was a Canda goosed flock. Things kept goin from sad to wurst

and tooday Elberta is a havnut provinss jist like Newfinland, and that Caligari Stampeed is maid up of Easterners cummin back hoam with nuthin more than ther ten-leeter hats to ther names.

Velda and Lamarr Hunsucker and their sacred—or is it Socred?—
cow.

icture the scene. A pair of straining Arabs (the four-legged kind) perspire noiselessly in rubber shoes as they pull a mowing machine across acres and acres of imported Kentucky bluegrass. The landscape is dominated by a Spanish *hacienda* in white adobe with a red tile roof. Beside the Moorish pool, nursing a sidecar, her silver-grey locks held back with combs and a mantilla, sits the owner of all she surveys, and more, much more. Granada? The highlands of Mexico? Even the Ewing Ranch, you may say? Try the Peace River country!

Velda Olds Hunsucker's spread seems to grow more extended every year. Her parents ("Folks, Val, jist plain folks like me," she twangs, clutching the joystick of her Rockwell Sabreliner) started with a small patch just off the Drumheller Badlands back in 1903.

Her father, Bowie "Shiv" Olds, had been a contract rider for the Bar Sinister out of Dallas, but strayed off the Chisholm Trail and lost his head—three hundred of them—in a snowstorm. He lost his other head when he saw Velda's momma getting sick on rotgut at Fort Whoop-Up. The experience turned both of them into lifelong teetotallers and vegetarians, the only ones west of Brandon at that time. They busted their collective sods to build a little substandard slab housing before baby Velda was born in 1904. ("I'ze barn a hole dam yare afore this blame province!" she whoops.)

Whence did the handle "Tex" arise? One would assume it was after she met her intended, Lamarr Culp Hunsucker of San Antonio. ("Naw, naw, Val, Sannintone!" she drawls.) But it was at school in Okotoks that she won the monicker. While other girls in deportment class carried books on their heads and tried to speak with a pickle up their palates, young Velda was slapping teachers on the back, talking louder than an auctioneer, and walking like a ranch-hand with haemorrhoids.

Steeped in Tom Mix and Hoot Gibson, Velda longed for Longhorns while her turnip-nibbling parents continued to woo

Marquis wheat. Daughter Tex waited for some "young Lockin-jaw" to take her out of all this. Alas, the only visitors were locusts from Lethbridge in 1934, and the family had to move to Turner Valley, where things took a turn for the worse. They found the roots of their first crop choked with sludge. Shiv Olds sold out to Candleoilco, and headed north to try again. He made a living for ten years at Leduc, then blew it again in '47. It was the same story next year in Redwater, and each time Imperial Oil bailed them out of the murk. By the time he was too old to raise anything much, he had more than a million acres in the Peace, but the reaper that mows us all overtook him after threescore and ten sections.

Meanwhile Tex was becoming a woman—well, sort of—and she knew she needed a pahdner for life. One day she was attending a peasant shoot on the Manic Estates, where they were releasing Spode seconds for the entertainment of the skeeters. The top gun seemed to be a long, horny-handed oilman who looked like Lyndon Johnson imagining he was John Wayne. Tex knew that in Lamarr Culp Hunsucker she had found her halter ego at last.

The wedding ceremony was conducted by a justice from the Peace, and the bride was given away, in the absence of both parents, by a wheat-pool cartel. The bride and groom left for a honeymoon in India under a procession of crossed Longhorns. ("Injure, hon, they got sum respeck for caows, there!" Lamarr explained.) While there they saw their dream house, and when they came back to live in Midnapore (Alberta, not India), Lamarr built Mrs. Hunsucker a complete replica, in Arborite, of the Taj Mahal.

Why didn't it last? (The marriage, not the Taj Mahal.) It depends whether one thinks that oil, cattle, or wheat is the glut issue in Alberta. After the honeymoon Velda lapsed into Eastern philosophy. She took to saying her mantra through speed traps and driving her Maserati in the Lotus position. Husband Lamarr swung the other way and became a convert to Western technology. Intimates started called the couple Tex and Hi-tex. Lamarr started a wide-open space program near Drumheller on the misunderstanding that the federal government's R and D program meant Research and Development, and not, as he later found, Rollback and Desist. He got impatient with this country's lack of desire to compete. Canadians were more interested in taking a chance on sure things like bingo and lotteries than in investing in enterprises with a high risk of return. Lamarr became disillusioned and started

Velda reigns as she pours.

investing his money south of the border. "Now you're acting like a true Canadian, darling," purred his bride.

The Hunsuckers' squabbles grew more and more nationalistic. Lamarr told Velda to stop wrapping her legs around her neck and saying those foreign words. She told him to tell his country to stop dropping acid rain. Their separation was solemnized shortly after the Quebec referendum in 1980 and was legalized in fifteen minutes in a Juarez court. The straw that snapped in hubby's mouth, Tex feels, was the National Energy Policy. Without a word, Lamarr hitched up his trousers, folded his big rig, and took everything back to San Antonio, Arborite Mahal and all. Rather than bribe her way into a green card, Tex watered a few stocks with her tears and decided to go back to the Peace she had known before marriage.

"The future of Alberta is in its past," Tex proclaimed, and with this simple declaration she sowed a million acres in wheat, joined the water lobby in Edmonton, and proved herself to be a source of irrigation to all. If one can't beat the government marauders, join them, preferably in a cartel, Tex reasoned. She got Jack Horner in her corner, went along with him on his China shopping expedition, and ended up pouring tea for Dung Chow Ping and Hoo Yoo Bang.

By now, the Chinese come directly to her for their wheat deals, and the Sino-Albertan signings are performed regularly on that endless lawn over cups of fragrant tea. While her province keeps breaking into its Big Pig Bank, Tex Hunsucker is breaking down the Great Wall of reserve with a product that comes out of the ground no more than four feet at a time, never blows its top, makes lots of bread, and doesn't require government funding.

There's only one problem. The lady doesn't know where she may have to move her spread next. Oil has just been discovered in the Peace.

"This is Calgary's Red Square, Val, and that's the Petro-Canada Building."

Berdish Columbya

This is eesily our most strikin province, anyways yuh look at it. This is a land of extreams, mountins and valleys, cappittle and laber. Ther don't seem to be no midseckshun in-between, fer to arbitchatrait tween the two. Now they are hagglin over ther big Expose to be flashed in 86 if it don't git 86ed by sum of them urbane gorillas. Oh theys a lotta high Roller-Roycers out here, but there's even more peeple out in the cold on park benches with brown bags, and it ain't their lunch, its their lugidge. Seems sumtimes more like Calcutter or Bumbay with all the socred cows runnin amuck amung yer Victorian birdcages.

The big munny used to be in yer forst industree, but both sides—the workers and the manidgemint—is too busy sawin away at eech other fer to cut much elts. Neether side kin seem to see yer woodwork fer yer trees. The only steddy piecework is them girls on the streets of Vancoovair, but there's jist as many I-rated sittyzens on the other corners with sines sayin "Flush the johns!"

I dunno wat Cussin Valery Rozedale wood makeout of all this, but the biggest trade in town is yer heroine bizness. It may be a shot in the arm fer the economee, but it sure seems to be a drug on the market. And all this in the most fotyjeenic sitty in the hole country. No wunder they is lookin over yer Rim fer sumthin elts to cum up.

Sum peeples say that Sociable Credit Card Billy Bennett is tryna bring Honky Kong here. His Opposit Posishun sez it alreddy is here, with swettyshops to keep peeple off the streets by day and rents so high it keeps them on the streets all nite. Watever elts it is, Bee Cee is the Last Chants Saloon fer anybuddy eest of here before they jumps offa yer Lyin Gait Bridge into yer Specific Ocean.

Prissy Wadsworth takes a tug in the right direction.

Priscilla "Prissy" Wayward Wadsworth

*P*rissy Wadsworth—what a conflicting swirl of values that fanciful name conjures up. Still the hardiest perennial bloomer in the Butchart Gardens set, Prissy is a source of inspiration to us all. As pilgrims yearn for their sacred city, be it Jerusalem, Mecca, or Salt Lake, so upper-class Canadian distaffers incline their long necks and aquiline noses each cocktail hour in the direction of this semiprecious city in a sylvan setting that is forever Anglo. Victoria is the Old Girls' Network's true capital, at present more Socred than sacred, but gardening, not government, is the chief growth industry. Even the standards of the street lamps are graced by baskets of flowers, so different from Vancouver, which continues to decorate its lamp-posts with the busy bodies of the oldest profession. (Actually, of course, gardening is the world's oldest profession, and unlike prostitution, it has been enhanced rather than spoiled by amateurs.)

Prissy Wadsworth is the reigning Queen Mother of this part of the Commonwealth, and she accepts the homage of her peeresses with a giggle, because her own family tree looks more like a stunted sapling. Perhaps this is why, with her multiple marriages, she has tried to cultivate a whole clump of them. Priss's great-grandmother, Eliza Scant, was a Cockney born within the sound of Bow Bells, one of a motley shipment of skivvies, tweenies, and scullery maids pressed into service in the 1850s and scattered among the *pukka sahibs** of Oak Bay.

Great-Grandmamma Eliza was so determined to swing her shift from downstairs to upstairs that she spent her days picking up fallen aspirates and cleansing her vowels. Eventually she got herself in the family way and ran off with the youngest black sheep of her employer's family, Ramsay Wayward. Instead of taking the Royal Road to a naval career, the young Ram set up in trade, and the

---

*Meens your uppity Berdish classes but sounds to me like a Injun gent throwin up.

result, of course, is merchandising history, as Wayward Department Stores continue to dot the landscape of Canada's West.

But it took another couple of generations of Waywards to go from the bray of Bow Bells to the precise patrician diction of Oak Bay. The result is the *lingua anglica* of our country, neither Mayfair nor Oxford, but possibly closer to Edinburgh at high tea. Every consonant emerges whole from between the teeth, and each vowel, free of glottal stops, can extend itself into a diphthong. Thus the plebeian "Canduh" becomes, in the Old Girls' mouths, the more mellifluous "Kyanadya." That extra diphthong identifies our class as surely as the erect carriage or the elongated narrow-gauge feet.

No one better typifies the very best we distaffers have to offer than Missillypriss, as she was dubbed by her schoolmates at Norfolk House and by her potential marital mates at Shawnigan Lake School for Boys. Both institutions of learning were dumbfounded when Priss skipped graduation to run off with Palmer Nimby Toole, scion of the Straits Tug and Ferry fortune. Pamby Nimby's papa, "Tug" Toole, scooped them out of their clandestine cubbyhole at the Empress Hotel, and with Priss in tow, had the knot securely tied at the end of the old Toole estate at Brentwood Bay, complete with a mass salute and hoot from the ferries at the bottom of their garden.

The marriage was only the first of several mergers. Eighteen years and four little Tooles later, Pamby slipped his moorings and headed for a permanent raunch in the Kootenays. Priss didn't mope in the mulch for a minute. She took over the push-pull business, bought up the Blackball Ferries in Seattle, and tried to do a deal with Premier Bigwhack Bennett. (He no longer believed in negotiating: Priss thinks he preferred to walk on water.) Instead, she ended up with the inter-island transport business in both Micro and Macronesia. Priss now runs her Pacific Rim affairs from a little Erik Arthurson glass house in Papeete, and has just sold a six-pack of tugs to Tonga, the new Empress requiring at least that many to get into her slip.

Prissy's three subsequent matrimonial ventures have only added to her current holdings. What turned out to be short-term leases with Paisley Hufty (helicopter logging), Beebe Shuve III (hard-pressed wood), and Bouvier Rill Wadsworth (Slabco post-stressed

AC or DC, this must be B.C.

housing) have merely served to solidify her four-ply empire—sorry, commonwealth.

It was Prissy who provided the economic spur to all four marriages; the quartet of husbands were content to let things ride, and all four have since been booted. She took her hard-pressed hubbies various wood products and began building her own fleet of sail-rigged motor ships, hedging her transport with wind power in case the ayatollahs of the world go cockamamie again. Already with good trades at her back she is saving thousands on the price of seagoing fuel. "First she takes the wind out of my sails, then she uses it to give herself a push with my purloined fortune," wails Beebe Shuve.

But the Wayward girl is a pioneer in the front line of a changing world economy. Even now, two-way trade on the Pacific Rim is outdoing any truck or trade we do with Western Europe. Prissy claims the time is short to beat the Yanks at their own game, and she's not talking baseball. Their game at the moment is "protection" for themselves while encouraging Canadians to become free traders. The term "protection" is never used, of course. It's "security of supply." That's how they shut us out of the bidding on their trillion (not bill, darling, trill) dollar defence budget after we'd spent five billion on their F-18 jet fighters.

Priss thinks we should be prepared to defend ourselves against the Americans and the Japanese, who have finally realized they should join up instead of beating each other to the punch. And Mexico is in on the merge too, just to keep up the interest on that loan. There are plants in Mexico and California turning out Chevrolets with Toyota engines. "Next it will be Volkswagen turning out Japanese Beetles!" Priss said with a grim laugh. "And what will they call GM after this? General Toy Motors? Can't you just hear Dinah Shore in the commercials urging us to see the U.S.A. in our Toyolettes!"

Canadians have one last chance, she feels. Expo 86. "If only we can avoid all those labour pains. As my old Mamma always said, it'll never heal if you picket." Friends and well-wishers are suggesting she move her offices from Victoria to Vancouver for the event, but Priss remembers all too vividly the earthquake of '46 when all the fish from the Stanley Park Aquarium ended up back in English Bay. I reminded her that the epicentre of the whole thing was at Courtenay on Vancouver Island, registering 7.3 on the Richter scale. But she reminded me that Mount St. Helen's is still showering its volcanic dandruff on Vancouver, not Victoria. Priss is quite an expert on the Richter scale, and not just because of her multiple marriages. Each point on that scale, she explains, increases the shakability factor exactly ten times. At 4.5 you're in for trouble. At 5.0 you will have to replace your crystal. At 6.0 you may have to buy new Limoges. And at anything over 7.0 you will be forced to purchase new lingerie.

Free, white-topped, and seventy-one, Priss divides her time between Papeete,* the Brentwood Bay mainstay, and a Sidney Spit retreat. She also mounts a one-person crusade against the Victoria male establishment, who consider her a chauvinist sow after some of her liberated antics. The Union Club on Humboldt Street is the last refuge of these old bastions, and the foot of woman has never tiptoed inside the doors of "Terminal City," as the club is called by insiders. Last year during the Royal visit, Priss persuaded her to unload her bouquet of Queen mums en route to christening a student sloop at Royal Roads. The flower deposition took only a few seconds, and there was no need to disturb the members. ("They are not dead, merely sleeping," Priss maintains.)

One of the older members caught a rearward glimpse of the Royal entourage as it streamed out the front door and complained to a bar steward that some damned female had been seen stuffing flowers into the spittoon in the lobby. When he was told that the intruder was Her Majesty, this old duffer sniffed fiercely and shuffled back to his chair, muttering: "By God, it's the thin edge of the wedge!"

Priss Wayward Toole Hufty Shuve Wadsworth has a word for such archaic attitudes: antidistaffestablishmentarianism.

---

*This is somewheres neer Nude Ginny where the Pope visited the lokel cannonballs.

Northwaste Terrortory

er yeers, all I bin heering about up Canda's frigid parts was yer Dome. Summers way up north ther was this big projeck that the guvmint was poring munny into, and nuthin ever seem to cum of it. Then the resta the country started doin it too. First there was yer Beezy Place with its big whoopee cushion. I seen it goin up slow on the TV and was mitey impress with the power of inflayshun in this country. Then Elberta announce a Saddledome fer the '88 Olimprick Games. It were call that cuz they wooden dip into ther Herniatage Fund, and the taxpayers was saddle with it. Then Ontaryario wanted one jist cuz B.C. had one first. Cuebec has had one fer years, but the Dome part is lyin on the ground beside the Olymphic Stayjum waitin fer the rest of the place to git finished. The reeson everybuddy sits on the edge of ther seets durin a game is not so much that the game is all that intrustin, but cuz they's no warshrooms in yet. It's not like Ontaryio: there's a place to stand, but no place to go.

But now Mizz Rozedale talks about this Dome up there in yer hardened Articks. It's a mistry to me how anybuddy kin make a livin offa snow and ice. I spend all winter cleerin the stuff off so's I kin git back to the land and scrape a livin. I never noo about these old gals trippin up to yer Tunderer fer to have seemenars, simposyums, and disgustin groops. She tells about cabbitches they grow up there in ther short seizins that is the size of baskyballs, and it takes no more time than for the wife and me and my boy Orville fer to git in the hay.

I'll tell yuh a secrit. I'm a thirty-second-degree Mason, but it jars the heck outa me to lern that them wimmen has a secrete sassiety of ther own. The wife, Valeda, has been threttenin to jine up, but I tole her that sted of freezin her bussle off in sum arctick spa, she shood be keepin the members glowin down here in Parry Sound.

Meg McAlpine, the force behind the worldwide Old Girls' spa network: Club Meg.

ast, but *certainly* not least, meet the legendary Meg McAlpine, the Dynasty Club's Great Dame. "Queenie" is truly Queen of the North, Head Mistress of the Canadian Powder Network. Some say she is the most influential woman in the country, especially since Margaret Trudeau married someone in trade.

Every summer, the girls get together up at Queenie's place to put their feet up, let their hair down, and talk shoppe. Now, Valerie Rosedale is no stranger to Powder Room Conferences, and I've knocked about with all of the Dynasty Clubbers at one time or another. I've rubbed elbows with jet-setters and had tea with the Queen, but an invitation to the Dynasty Club Dinner was an honour that little Valerie never expected in her wildest dreams.

Because of my position as editor-in-chief of this volume, many members were pressing for my ejection from the Distaffestablishment. The situation was certainly touch and go, and for weeks I savoured each Ladies' Club lunch as if it were my last. At the Garden Club, I had the feeling the flowers were for my funeral, and that one of the beds was being dug up for me. Idle fancy? Perhaps, but the thought of having my membership cut off made me quite faint. I became the Bridge Club dummy, which made me even more vulnerable. The Investment Club listed me as a liability. I got so teed off at the Golf Club, I left the straight and narrow and drove off. It seemed only a matter of time before I'd be expurgated by the Book Club. That would only leave curling—a chilling prospect.

Just in the nick of time, out of the blue came an invitation to the Dynasty Club Dinner. To dine with Queenie in her private pleasure dome! You could have knocked me over with a feather boa. The news spread like wildfire down the Powder Trail (the Old Girls' grapevine). The tide had turned in my favour, and I don't mind admitting that I lapped it up. "That Rosedale renegade" returned to her old haunts with head held high.

125

Now my only worry was how to prepare for the Big Event. I phoned Belle Barfman, knowing I could count on her for straight talk. All she said was "Come as you are!" When I pointed out that I was calling from the bathtub, and therefore felt obliged to discard her advice, Booby just laughed. Then I contacted Mazo Laroque-Fortier, who called me back from her Twin Otter in mid-flight. I thought perhaps she couldn't hear me over the roar of the engines, because every time I asked her what Meg looked like, she shouted, "I knew it!" I rang off in despair, packed my best cashmere twin sets, plaid skirts, and hiking boots, donned my mink coat, and headed up to Muskoka to hitch a ride with Biffy Blatta, that indefatigable Dynasty Clubber.

We took off in a spiffy powder-blue four-seater, the "Coup de Poudre." This means "the puff of powder," not to be confused with the *coup de foudre*, which is the clap of love at first sight. Biffy never goes anywhere without a couple of Goldens in the back seat. This time her pet favourites, Labatt and Brador, were our canine companions.

As we winged our way northward, I tried to pump Biffy, hoping for clues. So much has been said about Queenie and the meteoric success of her holding company, McEmpire Inc. Her international chain of ultra-exclusive holiday resorts, Club Meg, is just the tip of the iceberg. On Wall Street and on Bay Street, rumour is rife concerning her every move, but very little is known about the activities of McEmpire Inc. because Queenie owns all the shares.

Even less is known about the mysterious figure of Meg herself. Dubbed the Snow Queen by the press, she was even accused of being Howard Hughes by one enterprising pundit. Some experts, in all seriousness, have pegged her true age at two or even three hundred years. Despite her Scottish monicker, Establishment watchers have traced her roots to the highlands of Tibet and the Imperial Courts of China, Japan, and even ancient Egypt. No authenticated photographs of Meg are available, leading to the popular notion that she is a mistress of disguise, travelling the world freely while revealing herself only to the chosen few. Several *paparazzi** claim to have captured her on film, but none of the pictures has ever come out, giving rise to the persistent rumour that she is a witch with supernatural powers.

---

*Eyetalian flashers.

When I asked Biffy what Meg was like, she said, "You'll see!" I said that answer was even less helpful than Mazo's cryptic "I knew it." Biffy laughed like a drain. "Not 'I knew it,' Val—*Inuit*!" She chuckled for the rest of the trip.

Left to fly on the wings of my imagination, I tried to envision my first audience with Queenie. Expecting a venerable and ancient figure on a raised dais, cordoned off by rows of handmaidens, I planned to approach the Buddha-like presence with lowered eyes and mincing steps. Imagine my surprise, when we landed on an invisible airstrip in the middle of nowhere, to find that the sturdy figure in the parka who strode up to the plane was the legendary Meg McAlpine in person. She slapped me on the back and said, "Well, well, this must be our little deb from Debunk's!" I blanched and wilted slightly, but there was a twinkle in her eye.

Just then Carats and Brig breezed in from the southeast, with the heavily sedated Splits Puddock in tow. Heaven knows Splits can keep her head on the stormiest seas, when the rest of us look and feel like a tossed salad, but the dear girl hates to be airborne. As Splits puts it, "If God had meant Old Girls to fly, She would have given us feathers instead of furs!"

As we turned away, I was stunned to see that we stood not twenty yards from the entrance to Meg's dome, which was glittering in the sunlight. I hadn't noticed anything from the air except a wide expanse of tundra, with its seasonal cover of lavender, yellow, red, and blue flowers. How could I have missed it? Meg winked. "Let's just call it an ancient Inuit secret!"

Like all of the Club Meg "ARCs" (Arctic Recreation Centres), several of which I had visited in the past, Queenie's domed domicile is set right on top of a hot spring. This is where Old Girls gather to cleanse their pores, clear their heads, and trim their corpulent assets. It costs a small fortune to spend a week at a Club Meg, to be steamed, cured, and fed on *crudités*, but it's worth every penny. Presumably all of these pennies have dropped into Queenie's vaults, along with her legendary collection of rare artifacts.

"Welcome to my igloo, Val," said Meg. As I passed through the entrance I couldn't help letting out a gasp. Inside, the dome is a horticultural cornucopia. Rare and exotic plants of every description seem to flourish there, mingled with basic foodstuffs. Even the common cabbage grows to giant proportions under the constant exposure of the northern light. We wended our way in and out along a maze of pathways through such lush, dense greenery that at times we lost sight of the sky. Like Dorothy in the Land of Oz, I felt as though I had entered another world.

Rounding a particularly robust bougainvillaea, we found ourselves facing what looked like some kind of *art trouvé* fountain made from a giant's snowshoes. It turned out to be an elevator that operates on geyser power. As we descended in the cage, I could see Meg waving farewell from the top of the shaft. I had a sinking feeling. "What's up, girls?" I couldn't help inquiring.

"What's *down*, you mean. Don't get your knickers in a knot, Val," said Carats McBlythe. She and Brig had Splits propped up in a corner. "Meg has to nip off to Edmonton for a meeting. She'll be back in time for dinner. While she's away we'll have lots of time to freshen up and then show you around the place. We always start at the bottom and work our way up."

The elevator is on one side of a large open stairwell. As we went down, the bright sun faded to a dim twilight around us. We passed floor after floor of what seemed to be living quarters, then service quarters, then layer upon layer of what could only be storage space. Finally, as I was beginning to wonder if this was a journey to the centre of the earth, a glow from beneath us grew brighter and brighter, until we found ourselves in an enormous subterranean cavern. Now, I get claustrophobia just visiting the root cellar, but the vault of this natural rock formation was so incredibly high, and the space so brightly lit, with an Olympic-sized swimming pool at the bottom, that I felt as if I were at the beach.

In the pool, believe it or not, were the rest of the Dynasty Clubbers, paddling around with not a stitch on between them. As we stepped out of the elevator, I turned to Biffy and confided that I hadn't been skinny-dipping since summer camp, but as I hadn't packed a swimsuit for the Arctic, I would join the crowd in the altogether: "Which reminds me, Biffy, I left my suitcase in the plane under Brador's seat!"

The girls who overheard me seemed amused by this. "Not to worry, darling," said Biffy, "I didn't want to make you nervous by telling you before, but all Meg's ARC parties are strictly come-as-you-are. You never enter the ARC with any more than the clothes on your back, and you won't be needing those any more."

There was nothing for it but to dip into what turned out to be the experience of a lifetime.

On a Rolls, in the High—very High—Arctic.

Meg would be the first to admit that her empire is founded on water, "the greatest liquid asset the world has ever known." Every Club Meg is set on top of a natural spring, each quite distinct in character. I already knew from experience that Meg bubbles up the water at the Florida Club icy cold and crystal-clear. It heals sunburn, insect bites, and cuts and scratches, and makes your hair feel as soft as a baby duck's bottom. The water from this Arctic spring, on the other hand, comes up steaming hot, cloudy, and fragrant. After we'd undressed ourselves and Splits (no mean feat) and stretched her out on a deck-chair, Commie told me to pull the lever on a stand beside the pool. I did, and immediately a snow-storm fell on Splits's lifeless form. For a moment, there was silence, then came another flurry—this time of flailing Puddock arms and legs.

Though the sound was muffled by snow, her shrieks could have wakened the dead. "Not again! I told you never to do that again!" She leapt to her feet, wide awake now. "All right," said Splits, "who did it? *Who did it?!*" Need I mention who got fingered? Until that moment, I never knew I could do a back flip, but it's amazing what you can accomplish with a hundred and fifty pounds of Puddock charging straight at you.

The moment I hit the water I felt like a new Old Girl. I found I could float effortlessly, which was a blessing, because "the melting pot," as they call the pool, relaxed every fibre of this old string bean. It was so blissful, I could have stayed there forever. After-wards, we all stood in a bunch for the obligatory avalanche of snowflakes: all part of the Club Meg philosophy, apparently. It was certainly invigorating. This was followed by a mad dash to the rack of fluffy white bathrobes. Never let it be said that Old Girls aren't fast movers.

We piled into the elevator and headed back towards the earth's crust. I didn't see any buttons to push, but the contraption seemed to know where it was going. It stopped facing a long hallway. Each of the doors had a name on it. There must have been a mix-up, because after all the other girls had found their rooms, the only one left had "Valerie Farquharson" on it.

I went in anyway. Inside, I found a starkly furnished but charming compartment with a spectacular view of the stairwell. It consisted of bed, bathroom, and closet. Everything was white except for the Emily Carr* originals on the wall. In the closet I found only a white silk floor-length dress and a matching cap, which of course I put on.

No sooner had I dressed and restored my "starch and go" as best I could than there was a knock at the door. It was Biffy and Brig, come to take me on the grand tour. As we neared the elevator, the door opened and out stepped a portly Japanese gentleman in a grey pin-striped business suit. Neither of the other girls turned a hair, but I confess I was shocked. "I thought Club Megs were for girls only!"

"They are, Val," was Brig's casual reply. "That's just Queenie back from her business trip." I could see I had a lot to learn about the world of high finance.

---

*A paintin woman worked out in B.C. puttin swirls before pine.

Inflation has left the Right Wing up in the air.

We went to the "storage" levels I had noticed in passing on the first trip down the shaft. There wasn't time to view more than a fraction of Meg's collection, but even so it would take several volumes to describe all that I saw. Room after room opened to reveal a stunning array of jewellery, paintings, sculpture, antiques, and rare artifacts of every description. The library alone takes up two floors. Inuit art of course was abundant, and one room was devoted entirely to Bustelli of Nymphenburg pieces. The head of McEmpire Inc. is a passionate collector—partly out of a desire to conserve and protect our heritage, but also because she has no confidence at all in cold, hard cash.

And then it was time for dinner. I must say I was ravenous by this time, having nothing in my tummy since my breakfast bowl of bran and prunes. The long table, covered in exquisite white damask, was festooned with flowers. The table was set, and the wine glasses were filled, but I didn't see any sign of food. On each plate lay a stack of documents. The paper was very thick but quite translucent. The sheets seemed to be divided into sections, each one a different colour, with different-coloured print. I could see from the heading that this was the Dynasty Club's annual report. Naturally I swore up and down never to reveal its contents, and Val's word is her bond.

By this time all of the Dynasty Clubbers were assembled, each in a white silk gown and cap. I couldn't help noticing that my cap was the only one with a conical peak. Meg breezed in the door in an embroidered white silk kimono. "Sit down, girls, and tuck right in. We have a lot of information to go over here, and I want you to digest it thoroughly."

She wasn't kidding. After Prissy, the club secretary, had read the minutes of the last meeting, printed in yellow on green paper, everyone ate her copy. Trying to conceal my consternation, I took a tentative nibble. It tasted like steamed asparagus spears with hollandaise sauce! In fact, it was delicious.

We consumed each sheet as we went along. Each section of the report was read by the girl responsible for that ministry, as it were. At Meg's kind suggestion, I was dubbed "Mistress Without Portfolio." I can't remember exactly which course was what, but I think Splits's fisheries report was Arctic char with lemon and chervil, and I'm sure External Affairs was ratatouille. By the time we'd gone through the entire report my hunger pangs had gone, but I confess I was still a trifle peckish.

I don't want to leave you with the impression that gastronomic concerns were the main course of the evening's activities. Far from it. All the heady issues of the day were dealt with. I came away with much food for thought. By now, preparations for the Old Girls' international peace conference, to be held up at Meg's place, must be in full swing. All over the world, the silver-haired tea set are busy as beavers, trying to preserve the planet from the pickle it's in.

Without women like Meg McAlpine, the world would be a sorry place indeed. If I can put this book behind me and start again with a clean slate, perhaps I will be invited back some day as a full-fledged Dynasty Clubber.

"Pull, Jarvis, pull: that's what got us where we are today."

III

The Honours Missed

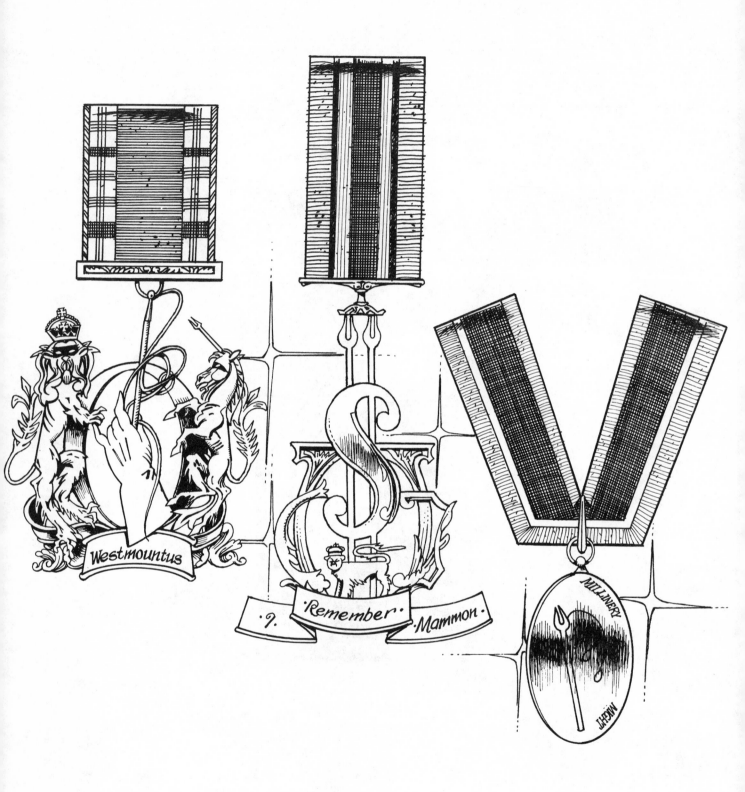

Westmountus

I Remember Mammon

MILLINERY

The New Orders

When I was a maiden, before I completely lost my head, the only commodity a female had to market was her honour. Nowadays, as my daughter Stephanie is only too eager to tell me, the game has changed. One's honour, it seems, is no longer a mark of anything, and what was once a preferred stock-in-trade in the marital market-place has given way to more common forms of sharing. Honour goes the way of all flesh, eventually, and most of us have the stretch marks to prove it, but at least in my day it was a highly negotiable commodity, not just a blanket overnight pass.

It was also at one time possible in this country to prove beyond any doubt that one was a lady with a capital L. If one's husband was offered, or even bought, a knighthood, he was addressed as Sir by more than the household servants, and his Lady lucked in too. Sir Robert Borden put a stop to such honours in 1919, after he had safely gotten his, you will notice. Now there were to be no more knights across the board, only rooks, pawns, and the odd bishop. But in 1931, Prime Minister R. B. Bennett, the only man to greet the Great Depression in top hat and claw-hammer coat, allowed us our titular jollies again and a few more gaudy knights flourished amid the fiscal gloom.

But alas, the interregnum was short-lived, and knighthood was deflowered again in 1936. This came just in time to ruin the last chance we Canadians had of rising above our American neighbours. It was that little sonofa son of a son of a renegade, Mackenzie King, who hopelessly democratized us once and for all, at the same time retaining his own title as King of the Commons for the next quarter of a century.

Let's face it. The Old Boys have made a mess of it. It's time for the Old Girls to go back to the Honours system.

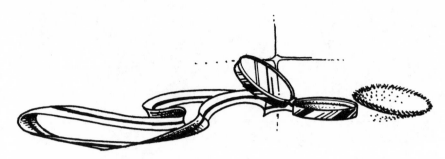

THE ORDURE OF CANADA

What a fertile field this conjures up for the symbol-minded! Women have been digging the dirt (and often been treated like it) ever since we were evicted from that first male sanctuary, the Eden Centre. Thrust out into the wilderness, it was woman, not man, who made a garden bloom again. By smoothing it in the bush, we have never thrown in the trowel or turned our backs on our roots.

Man, on the other hand, has frittered away his time in the filthy business of politics and still insists on putting his foot in it. We women do the same with the Real Thing and come up smelling like roses. The hand that rocks the cradle also trims the hedge, and we act as the true cultivators of our heritage by continuing to turn our cold frames into hot beds.

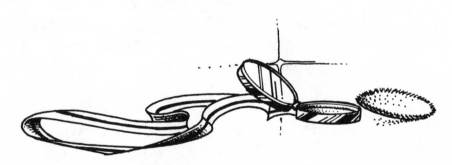

THE ORDEAL OF THE SHIV

This is a non-volunteer award that represents one of the back orders on the dark side of the ledger. There comes a tide in the affairs of men when they revert to a condition that can only be described as the boyopause. This is the time of the change of life-style when members of the Old Boys' Network start to think about turning in their forty-year-old model for a pair of brand-new twenties.

Recent legislation has made divorce a no-fault proposition, as blameless as a fender-bender in a parking lot. Now that divorce means never having to say you are sorry, we can expect more and more of our sex to become the titular heads of the household, after being under wedlock and key for most of our productive years. Personally I preferred our old biblical notion of original sin, which made both parties feel guilty even before they began.

But divorce suits turn out to be much more expensive than wedding trousseaus, and recent legislation coming out of Alberta gives us a fifty-fifty chance of eventually getting custody of the money. There is a magical power in those three little words, "conjugal community property," and the Ordeal of the Shiv can be a two-sided affair.

Recipients of this award are entitled to call themselves Grand Cross Dames of the Order of the Double Cross, and to be compensated in perpetuity.

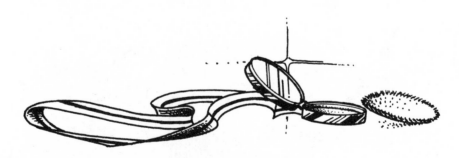

THE ORDERLY OF THE HOSPITALLER

This order preserves the hostel attitude of the Middle Ages, and volunteers are expected to take orders instead of giving them for a couple of hours three afternoons a week. In devoting their time to such charitable work, Grand Cross Dames often serve the afflicted as a form of occupational therapy, in the absence of any husband to complain about. The highest order of service performs the lowest work and attains the rank of Admirable, in charge of all the vessels on one's particular floor. Carrying the can for man often engenders mixed feelings and often leads to a withdrawal from the everyday world, into one of pure contemplation with no further orders.

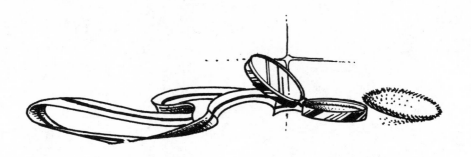

THE MOST VULNERABLE ORDER
OF ST. JOHN'S AMBIVALENCE

St. John, of course, was the first Baptist to lose his head over a table dancer, and this Ambivalent order is open to those distaffers who have mixed feelings about the beast that has just left their lair. The order is worn on the sleeve with a plain black ribbon, which can also be used as a tourniquet in first-aid classes.

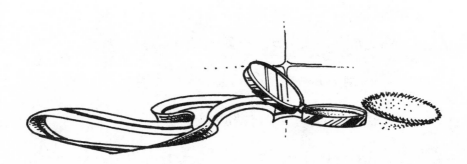

THE SECOND ORDER OF LAZARUS

Membership is raised by invitation only, but during leap year this cuts both ways. Lazarus is the patron saint of social lepers, who regain their status in society by becoming born again into the marital market. Old Girls ready for a second round consider this order to be a Grand Priority, and the insignia is a Maltese Cross worn under the third knuckle of the left hand.

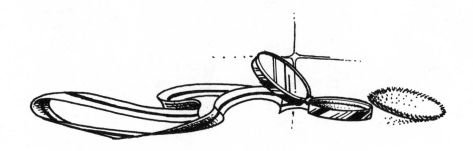

THE ORDER OF MILLINERY MERIT

One of the Powder Network's highest accolades is the Order of Millinery Merit, given to Old Girls who really know how to use their noggins. Its recipients are the crowned eggheads of Canada, and indeed the world, for this is an international honour.

A man takes his hat off to pay his respects, while a lady puts on her best bonnet. The bigger the bash, the bigger the beanie, we always say! For the Queen's Plate or any jewel in the Triple Crown, the Powder Brokers' pates fairly burst into bloom. Men may be amused by such millinery flamboyance, but they would gladly stick tulips in their toques if they thought it would help them pick the right ponies. The poor boys have tried homburgs, berets, peaked caps, top hats, and fedoras, but no haberdasher can help them. Meanwhile, Old Girls with flower-beds on their heads keep on pocketing the purses. Of course, Queen Mums don't have to queue up to cash in, so don't bother sticking around the wicket hoping for a hot tip.

I can't deny that our Blue Bonnet track record is uncanny, but there's nothing fishy about it. When an Old Girl says she's going to put her thinking cap on, she means it. The thinking cap is one of the greatest Old Girl gizmos of all time, and it really works, if you know how to use your head. For some reason men have never been able to get the hang of it.